THE CRISIS OF
HOMOSEXUALITY

THE
CRISIS OF
HOMOSEXUALITY

EDITED BY
J. ISAMU YAMAMOTO

VICTOR BOOKS®

A DIVISION OF SCRIPTURE PRESS PUBLICATIONS INC.
USA CANADA ENGLAND

Unless otherwise noted, all Scripture quotations are from the *Revised Standard Version*, © 1946, 1952, 1971, Division of Christian Education, National Council of Churches of Christ in the United States of America. Other quotations are from the *King James Version.* ˠ

Cover illustration: Ronald Chironna

Library of Congress Cataloging-in-Publication Data

The Crisis of Homosexuality / edited by J. Isamu Yamamoto.
   p. cm.
     ISBN 0-89693-283-4
     1. Homosexuality—Religious aspects—Christianity.
  I. Yamamoto, J. Isamu
     BR115.H6C75   1990
     261.8′35766—dc20   90-41673
                                           CIP

1 2 3 4 5 6 7 8 9 10 Printing/Year 94 93 92 91 90

CONTENTS

PREFACE

Because of the explosive nature of this topic, let us begin by setting the proper context for this book.

First, *we are all human beings*. That is to say, there is no such phenomenon as "a homosexual." There are only people—human persons—made in the image and likeness of God, yet fallen, with all the glory and the tragedy which that paradox implies, including sexual potential and sexual problems. However strongly we may disapprove of homosexual practices, we have no liberty to dehumanize those who engage in them.

Second, *we are all sexual beings*. Our sexuality, according to both Scripture and experience, is basic to our humanness. Angels may be sexless; we humans are not. When God made humankind, he made us male and female. So to talk about sex is to touch a point close to the center of our personality. Our very identity is being discussed, and perhaps either endorsed or threatened. So the subject demands an unusual degree of sensitivity.

Third, *we are all sinners*, indeed (among other things) sexual sinners. "I doubt if there is anyone who has not had a lustful thought that deviated from God's perfect ideal of sexuality," wrote Dr. Merville Vincent of the Department of Psychiatry at Harvard Medical School. Nobody (with the sole exception of Jesus of Nazareth) has been sexually sinless. There is no question, therefore, of coming to this book with a horrid "holier-than-thou" attitude of moral superiority. Being all of us sinners, we stand under the judgment of God and we are in urgent need of the grace of God.

"Homophobia," or the attitude of personal hostility towards homosexual persons, is a mixture of irrational fear, hatred, and even revulsion. It overlooks the fact that the great majority of homosexual people are not responsible for their condition (though they are, of course, for their conduct). Since they are not deliberate perverts, they deserve our understanding and compassion, not our rejection. No wonder Richard Lovelace calls for "a double repentance," namely "that gay Christians renounce the active lifestyle" and that "straight Christians renounce homophobia."

At the heart of the homosexual condition is a deep loneliness, the natural human hunger for mutual love, a search for identity, and a longing for completeness. If homosexual people cannot find these things in the local "church family," we have no business to go on using that expression. The alternative is not between the warm physical relationship of homosexual intercourse and the pain of isolation in the cold. There is a third alternative—namely a Christian environment of love, understanding, acceptance, and support.

I do not think there is any need to encourage homosexual people to disclose their sexual orientation to everybody; this is neither necessary nor helpful. But they do need at least one confidant to whom they can unburden themselves, one who will not despise or reject them but will support them with friendship and prayer. They may also need some professional, private, and confidential pastoral counsel; possibly the support of a professionally supervised therapy group; and many warm and affectionate friendships with people of both sexes.

Same-sex friendships are to be encouraged, like those in the Bible between Ruth and Naomi, David and Jonathan, and Paul and Timothy. There is no hint that any of these was homosexual in the erotic sense, yet they were evidently affectionate and (at least in the case of David and Jonathan) demonstrative. Of course, sensible safeguards will be important. But in African and Asian cultures it is common to see two men walking down the street hand in hand, without embarrassment. It is sad that our Western culture inhibits the development of rich same-sex friendships by engendering the fear of being ridiculed or rejected as a "queer."

Perplexing and painful as the homosexual Christian's dilemma is, Jesus Christ offers him or her (indeed, all of us) faith, hope, and love—the faith to accept his standards and his grace to maintain them, the hope to look beyond present suffering to future glory, and the love to care for and support one another.

—John Stott

FOREWORD

When I was managing editor for a publishing house in San Francisco several years ago, I found that I was the only straight male on the staff. As a matter of fact, the publisher and the president of the company were lovers—the president being my immediate superior.

You would probably assume that since I am a conservative Christian I was constantly filled with disgust in that environment. Only once, however, did I feel such revulsion. It was when I answered the phone for one of my associates. The caller asked in what can only be called the stereotypical gay voice, "Hi, I'm Tom's lover. Is he there?" What jarred me was that although I knew Tom was gay, his voice and behavior betrayed no hint of his sexual orientation. Tom's manner shattered one of many false impressions I had of gay people. It did not, however, quell the nausea I felt for homosexual behavior.

"Love the sinner, but hate the sin" is a frequent (and often trite) Christian admonition. But in my experiences at this publishing house, I did come to care for many of the people I worked with. I also felt deep sadness for them since this was a time when AIDS was just beginning to rock the gay community. And yet, I did not have the same feelings for all of them. Some were self-centered, materialistic, and ruthless. I admit, they irritated me. Others, like Tom, were warm, witty, and generous. I always enjoyed their company.

John was another person I got along well with. He was a part-time freelancer, who worked on data entry for the business department after hours. Since I often worked late into the evening, we would occasionally be the only ones in the office. That gave us time to chat. Our conversations often centered on baseball—he was a San Francisco Giants fan and I was an Oakland A's fan. One night, I intentionally sought him out, having heard the A's had won and the Giants had lost. I was about to razz him when I saw that he was perturbed. I sat down next to him and asked what was wrong. He turned toward me with a terribly sad look on his face and said, "I had my blood tested, and I just learned this afternoon that I have AIDS."

As his hands shook on his lap, tears formed in his eyes. I wanted to reach out and touch him—to tell him how sorry I felt for him. But, at that time, I knew so little about AIDS, except that it was contagious, fatal, and without remedy. I could not stretch out my hand. And, because I could not touch him, only inane words dribbled out of my mouth.

This book you hold in your hands has special meaning for me because its authors have taught me a great deal about homosexuality, about common diseases in the gay community, and, most important of all, about people who are struggling with their homosexuality.

In these pages, Darlene Bogle and Colin Cook share the bitter experiences that drove them to homosexuality, and of Christ's compelling love that drew them to God. Bob Davies relates the victories, and the defeats, of how one ex-gay ministry—Exodus—has grown into an international network of ministries. Journalist Tim Stafford and sociologist Ronald Enroth examine the broad array of ex-gay and prohomophile ministries.

Proctologist Bernard Klamecki describes the physical damage and diseases that might be incurred from homosexual activity. Biblical scholar Ronald Springett reviews the conflicting positions on the scriptural references to homosexuality and offers his own conclusions. Psychologist Stanton Jones surveys what behavioral science actually says about sexual orientation and gives us invaluable insights on how we should minister to gays.

Christianity Today's managing editor, David Neff, explores the implications of the sexual-addiction movement for ministry to homosexuals and poses questions we need to consider. Pastor-scholar John R. W. Stott provides a moving preface to this book. Special thanks are due him for allowing us to adapt an excerpt from his book *Involvement* (Old Tappan, N.J.: Revell, 1985).

These people have not only informed me, but they have inspired me to reach out and touch with Christ's healing love those whom I once regarded as untouchable. I pray this book will do the same for you.

—*J. Isamu Yamamoto*
Christianity Today Book Editor

Chapter 1

HEALING FROM LESBIANISM

Darlene Bogle

Tears scalded my cheeks. A large knot in my throat refused to move no matter how hard I swallowed. The headlights from oncoming traffic blurred like a merry-go-round fantasy ride as I sped around the mountainous curves.

God, we've been around this mountain before! My thoughts argued with the feelings of conviction in my heart. *I can't change my homosexuality. I've tried before. It just doesn't work. I still like women!*

For seventeen years I had struggled with lesbianism. I never really believed that I was "born that way," but it sure seemed easier to live in cowboy boots and Levi's than in high heels and lace.

When I was a teenager, I committed my life to Christ, yearning to serve him. I wanted to become all Scripture said I could be. I longed to live out my faith with a wholeness I saw in others. Yet, my relationship with Christ was constantly at odds with the lesbian lifestyle I had entered in my teenage years. I didn't want to give up either of them, and yet I was unable to be at peace in either world. Christianity and homosexuality caused such an inner turmoil that I felt as if I was being torn apart.

While tears flowed down my cheeks, I whispered aloud, "Okay, God, I'll try it one more time. If your word is true, then show me there is healing from my childhood pain and victory over my homosexual yearnings."

Childhood beginnings

As twins, my sister and I surprised and overwhelmed our mother who was expecting just one baby as a playmate for her sixteen-month-old son. With three small children to care for by herself, it was no wonder she soon followed my alcoholic and usually absent father to the bars, frequently leaving us with sitters.

The affects of alcohol shattered my life long before I was old enough to understand. I had just turned one when I became a victim of incest. While my father was drunk, he turned a time of playful activity into betrayal and sexual abuse. Years later, I can still hear him say to my mother, "She'll never remember. She's too little for it to matter."

But it did matter. Also, it was the first of many sexual-abuse events in my life. I was almost three when the boyfriend of one of our babysitters violated me sexually. When I was eight, an older boy in the neighborhood, who decided I should be shown the things that big people do, ravished me. I was ten the year a man at the playground selected me to molest. At thirteen, another neighborhood boy, who had a party at his home while his parents were gone, violently raped me.

When I was five, my parents divorced, and my mother married a man who disliked children and who was also an alcoholic. Although Frank did not sexually abuse me, he subjected all of us to his drunken tirades on a regular basis. He frequently stormed through the house, picking up our clothes or school books and throwing them out the back door. When we went to retrieve them, he would lock us out, cursing and calling us vulgar names. He either refused to buy food or, after he did go grocery shopping, belittled us as we ate. He regularly attacked Mom both verbally and physically. I often lay awake at night, unable to sleep until Mom was home safe from the tavern. When the fighting started, I plotted how I would kill Frank— once I was big enough.

But something happened that convinced me that physical strength could not answer my life's battles. After we moved next door to a Free Methodist Church, I developed a friendship with the pastor's children, who were close to my age. Because of the violence in my home, I retreated to the church for peace and love. For the first time, I saw parents who spent time with their children and prayed with them. They also asked me to join in their daily prayer time, and they found ways to involve me in the Sunday-school programs.

I was sixteen when they took me to a high-school youth camp, where I received Jesus as my Savior. I was immediately over-whelmed with a love that had been nonexistent in my family life. I had struggled with the concept of a heavenly Father who would love and protect me when all I had known in my life were fathers who had abandoned or victimized me. But now I was thrilled to have Jesus as my friend.

And yet, a nagging loneliness consumed me at the core. Even as a Christian, I could not relate to most church people. My childhood had built a chasm of isolation that even my newfound faith in Jesus did not seem to span. I had spent years building emotional defenses for survival in a home that lacked nurturing, that was void of positive role models and void of love. I was unsure how to embrace the very thing I longed for most: the acceptance of others that would help me accept and love myself.

The Christian college experience
Since my pastor's wife had encouraged me to attend a Christian school, I decided to enroll with a missions major and use my background to help others. But almost from the first week on campus it was obvious I was the one who needed help.

I felt out of place and terribly lonely. I often considered suicide. Almost daily I visited Marie Hollowell, the dean of women, who listened to me and prayed with me. She was unaware that she was my touchstone of Christian reality. I felt if I could tell her all the garbage inside me, unload the hurting and ugliness of rejection and rape, and if she still loved me, then perhaps I could believe God really did care for me.

In the process of sorting out the old pain, a new issue developed. Lance, a boy from my religion class, asked me to go out with him. He was a great-looking guy and the son of a prominent minister. We dated several times, mostly to church or services where he was one of the student speakers. We took long walks around campus and talked late into the night. I was falling in love with someone who liked me and had even said he loved me. My wall of isolation was on the verge of crumbling.

One night we made our way to the basement of the chapel on campus, where we could keep warm and talk in private. I sensed this was a special night, as Lance had mentioned he didn't want anyone to know where we were, and he had something important to tell me. We stood in the darkness, his arms wrapped around me. He pulled me closer and kissed me gently.

"I do love you, Darlene." He paused. "Do you love me?"

My heart was pounding as I whispered back, "Yes, I really do."

His heavy breathing almost frightened me. "Then prove it to me. Prove how much you love me, Darlene," he said. "Have sex with me."

I jerked away in shock. "What?" I stared at him in disbelief.

"I want to make love with you," he said, reaching for me.

My mind snapped. "You're a Christian! You even preach that sex before marriage is a sin!" I turned away and rushed for the door. "You're no different from non-Christian guys. At least they tell you up front that all they want is sex!"

Tears stung my eyes as I raced across campus. When I saw light in Dean Hollowell's apartment, I rushed to her door. She took one look and invited me in, where I shared the events that had occurred with Lance. With clenched teeth, I vowed never to trust another man— not even a Christian man!

Dean Hollowell became more like a mother to me in the following months. With her I felt safe, and she always made time to listen to me. Through her counseling I began to understand how my childhood influenced the way I reacted as a young adult. She spent hours teaching me about God as a loving Father who would take care of me and help me become more than a product of a bad environment.

I commenced my second year of college with renewed hope that what I had experienced in life would be used to help others, and that someday I would overcome my isolation and loneliness. It was then that I met a girl who was moving into the dorm room I had occupied all summer. Barbara was tall and slender with velvet black hair. She was from a Christian home and had been active in church all her life. She was charged with an electric personality, and we hit it off immediately. Although we were inseparable during that semester, sharing about our home lives and future dreams, she always seemed guarded in what she said about friends from her hometown. Then, as Christmas vacation was approaching, she shared her deepest secret with me.

"Darlene, I won't be coming back to school next semester." She paused. "There is something I want to tell you."

She shared in depth about her involvement with homosexual women, and how she discovered that she was a lesbian. She said she really cared for me and would miss me. I questioned her about being a Christian and a lesbian. She said she felt she could be both, and that God accepted her. The arguments she provided sounded logical, and subtly I was seduced into a physical relationship with her. Although the Bible said it was wrong, I felt more love and acceptance from my relationship with her than I had with any boy I had dated. While my inner conflict raged, there were times I didn't even care if God said it was a sin. I loved Barbara, and she loved me. But then she went away, and I was alone again.

I called her every day during the Christmas break. I planned to work through the New Year's holiday and then spend a few days with her before classes resumed. I received a call, however, that shattered my life. Barbara's mother told me that Barbara had taken an overdose of pills. Barbara was dead.

Once again I ran to Dean Hollowell's apartment, tears and rage spilling out together. I shared the entire story with her, confessing our sexual involvement. I tried to justify our actions because of our love, but inside I knew it was a sin.

"I love you, Darlene, and so does Jesus. He will never reject you, and one thing you can count on—I won't reject you until Jesus does! But you do know that this is no more acceptable to God than having sex with Lance."

I felt so loved and accepted as she held me close. I blinked back the tears and nodded my silent agreement. Her voice continued in the same whisper: "Jesus, we ask you right now to bring healing into Darlene's life. I don't know how you are going to do it, but we just ask you to perform one of your miracles. We praise you, Jesus, and we ask this in your name."

Other staff members at the college did not mirror her loving acceptance. As word spread about Barbara's death and our relationship, many of the residence counselors pushed for my expulsion. "Her case is too difficult," stated one instructor. "We cannot be expected to deal with someone who is homosexual."

Although Mrs. Hollowell chose to listen to the inner voice of the Lord and allowed me to remain in school, I sensed a growing rejection from faculty and friends as I tried to work through my emotions. I thought about running away from God—and from Christian condemnation—but I could not escape the awareness of God's love and the prayers of a woman who said she would love and accept me as long as Jesus did.

A few weeks later, I learned she had accepted a position with an American university in Beirut, Lebanon. I was devastated. Once again, I felt abandoned.

Joining the lifestyle

After I quit college and moved to California where no one would know me, I began to frequent the gay clubs. I thought if I could submerge myself in the homosexual lifestyle, I could remove the pangs of guilt. Meanwhile, it was obvious to the older patrons I was not only new in town, but was a "kid." They felt it was their responsibility to care for me. I enjoyed the popularity and the new sense of acceptance.

Almost every night I got drunk. And, although someone always managed to get me home safely, the following night I'd be back repeating the scenario. Since alcohol did not drown out all my conflicts, I started to mix pills and smoke a few joints to forget everything except the present moment. I felt as if I had finally succeeded in putting God out of my life. Ironically, however, barroom discussions turned to religion. After I told them about my life at a Christian college, several of them echoed my experiences.

We often discussed Scripture, and how a loving God could "make us this way, then say homosexuality is a sin." More than one Bible-school dropout lamented that Christianity didn't seem to work in this area of sexuality. John, "the Preacher," voiced the feelings most like my own: "I know it's wrong, but right now, I don't care what God thinks. I've tried to make Christianity work, and I just can't." Margaret, on the other hand, voiced the more common feeling: "I think God made us gay, and he doesn't expect us to change. We need to learn to accept ourselves and our sexuality. God doesn't care who you love as long as you don't hurt anyone."

Inside my heart, I heard, "Darlene, I love you. I want to make you whole." I knew I was wrong, but I couldn't seem to change. I knew that inner voice was God's way of answering Marie Hollowell's prayers. One night I was in a bar, sick inside because of the emotional conflict. That voice kept saying, "Darlene, I love you. I have chosen you. I will not leave you alone." I silently countered the statement. *But I've tried to change. I can't! I hate men, and you take away every woman I love.*

I put my head on the bar and closed my eyes. *God, why can't I just forget about you? Why can't I get drunk enough to never hurt again?* My mind whirled with questions, especially why Barbara had died and why Dean Hollowell had left me alone. I could hear the words she had whispered so many times. "I'll always love you, Darlene. I will never reject you. Jesus is committed to your wholeness." Somehow I felt hope when I thought about Mrs. Hollowell. *Maybe I could change.* I bit my lip to stop the tears. *No, I tried before, and failed.*

The bartender interrupted my inner conflict by tapping my shoulder: "Come on, Darlene. Head off the bar. You've had too much to drink."

I lifted my head and met her gaze. "I'm not drunk. I wish I were." I shook my head. "I'm just trying to forget how much God loves me."

A return
If I could not run from God, perhaps I really could change by running to him. And so, I decided to leave the homosexual lifestyle and return to church.

I found a Bible-believing, evangelical congregation in my neighborhood. I read Scripture aloud, submitting my life anew to Jesus and asking for strength. I worked at reprogramming my mind with Christian music and hearing the Bible on tape. But almost daily I struggled with images in my head that came to tempt me back to the gay lifestyle. Although I built a wall of protection to drown out the inner voices that said I could never change, I knew I needed help.

After attending a few Sunday services, I made an appointment with the pastor. I knew I needed considerable prayer if I were to overcome this spiritual stronghold of homosexuality in my life. I met with the pastor and briefly explained the circumstances in my life that had brought me to the San Francisco Bay Area. I had been away from a Christian environment for two years, yet the longing to be whole was stronger now than ever. I confessed my involvement with homosexuality. I asked for special prayer that God would remove these feelings.

The pastor's response was one I would hear from others over the next fifteen years. "I don't know how to help you," he said. "But I will pray for you. I've never yet seen a homosexual change for any length of time, so I don't give you much hope."

His platitude shattered my heart, and resentment erupted. I vowed never to ask for help again. Why had I expected the same support and hope that Dean Hollowell always provided?

He put me on a year "spiritual" probation before he would even consider me for church membership. My goal of proving him wrong became the focus of my existence. I would not only become a church member, I would prove to him that homosexuals could change. I would never let him say to another person that he did not know anyone who had changed. I would beat the odds!

The year passed quickly, and I did all the right things. I attended every service, even midweek. A year later, the pastor officially welcomed me into membership. I thought I had beaten the odds, but I never felt accepted at his church. I had done all the right things. But inside I was as lonely as I had been in the bars. At least when I was out drinking, I did not have to go home alone—I almost always went home alone from church. The singles of the congregation were either too old or too young. The Sunday-school classes were geared to young couples, and the church events revolved around families. The holiday celebrations were so painful as I watched traditional families celebrate that I retreated to my apartment and stayed in bed for the weekends of Thanksgiving and Christmas. Although I was in a "church family," no one ever took me home to share in the family together times.

I started dropping by the gay clubs in the afternoon between Sunday services. Before long, I discontinued attending the evening service. Shortly afterwards, I met a woman from a town several miles south of Oakland, and I decided to move where I was wanted and accepted. Of course, I never told the pastor why I was moving. I called it a job transfer. I thought I could fade away without any confrontation.

As soon as I started my new job, however, I realized God still had his hand on my life. There were five women who worked in the office and were supporting their husbands through Bible college. I was not left off the hook. Although I was sure my former pastor would not learn about my return to the gay lifestyle, I was still concerned that I would not become one more statistic to prove to him that homosexuals cannot change.

Once again, I submerged myself in the homosexual lifestyle. I became active in gay politics. It was the early 1970s, and gay rights were moving to the front pages of newspapers across the land. It started with the Stonewall event in New York, and now California was to have its first Gay Pride week with a parade in San Francisco, where I helped to organize and promote the events.

Although I found acceptance in the gay community, there was one issue I could not resolve or accept. The Metropolitian Community Church, with its message of God's unconditional acceptance of homosexuality, gnawed at me during the parade. I refused to walk anywhere near their massive float. God and my gayness were at odds. Although I attempted to numb the conflict with alcohol and drugs, I could not rid myself of the longing for a close relationship with Jesus Christ. The next three years were an endless treadmill of activity, trying to forget God, but still hearing his voice in my heart, calling me to try again.

A second attempt for change

I unsuccessfully ignored God. Christian co-workers often confronted me about my behavior, but even more often the Holy Spirit convicted me. I was not happy in the gay lifestyle because I knew God was not pleased with homosexual behavior. Although part of me wanted acceptance, another part of me wanted to change. And so, I decided to try one more time to see if God could still my inner turmoil.

I discovered a small church where no one knew about my background. I signed up for classes at a Christian college. If I returned to my education and prepared myself to enter the ministry, perhaps my conflicts would cease. I prayed the same prayer every day for months: "This time, Lord, let me find out how to make Christianity work for me."

As the weeks passed, I was fairly consistent in my "white knuckle" Christianity. I was determined to make things work out this time. I only had one problem—it was difficult to keep my thoughts under control and to stay away from gay friends. I worked with some gay men, lived in an apartment with several gay couples, and because I was well known in the gay community, I ran into old friends no matter where I went.

After a friend suggested Christian counseling as an option for dealing with some of my emotional issues, I contacted a ministry that specialized in ex-gay counseling in Los Angeles. I made a special trip just to meet with their leaders. From the time I walked into their office, however, I was uncomfortable. I sensed they did not have any more answers than I had. I took their material, asked a few leading questions, and walked out more depressed than ever. I did not need platitudes of how capable God was to perform miracles. I needed to see a miracle lived out in someone's life.

I searched the Christian bookstores for material that would offer hope and tell of even one person who had changed. What I found were books by psychologists and theologians explaining why people turn to homosexuality and God's aversion to that behavior. I could not accept what they were saying as God's answer. If he were going to send me to hell for being what I could not help, then he was not a just God.

Despite being discouraged, I continued to seek help. I went to a Christian therapist, talked to secular counselors, found a couple of personal testimonies from "anonymous" people who said they had been healed from homosexuality, but I could not find one person who could tell me firsthand of having experienced healing.

I regained some hope when I read 1 Corinthians 6:11: "And that is what some of you were. But you were washed, you were sanctified, you were justified in the name of the Lord Jesus Christ and by the Spirit of our God." If there were help and healing for the Corinthian Christians, then there must be healing for my sexual brokenness.

One Christian counselor helped me deal with the issues of incest and rape that had occurred during my childhood. I had repressed memories and emotions connected to these events because I could not change the fact that they had happened. During times of therapy, I saw that my anger toward and competitiveness with my father and other males, as well as my aversion to intimacy, were rooted in these experiences of abuse. Up until that time, I had not tried to sort out those repressed memories and emotions and find healing.

Nevertheless, I did not realize that I could never turn from the destructive patterns of lesbian behavior until I faced the effects of being victimized. The traumatic events of my childhood had directly influenced the wholeness I had been seeking in my relationship with Christ. The void of nurturing and parenting from my early years had left me emotionally unfulfilled, although outwardly I appeared independent and strong.

Therefore, I could not resist the magnetic pull back to homosexual behavior. Once again I left the church and returned to the gay clubs. I wanted a lifestyle where I was accepted. God seemed too distant, almost taunting me with a promise of hope that was always just beyond my reach. I vowed not to be committed to him or to anyone else again. My use of drugs, alcohol, and sexual promiscuity increased with multiple relationships. I resolved that if I were going to hell for being gay, I might as well not embrace any moral standards.

In my rebellion against God, I stole large sums of money from the convenience store where I worked evenings. Although I took the polygraph and voice stress analyzer tests along with other employees, I was not discovered, while several of my co-workers failed the tests. I had not only become a compulsive thief, I had become a compulsive liar. 1 Timothy 4:2, ". . . whose consciences have been seared as with a hot iron," passed through my mind. I justified my behavior, rationalizing that if God would not back up his word about truly setting someone free (John 8:36), then I might as well do whatever I wanted in order to take care of myself.

Beyond my ability

And then, I was faced with a situation that money and manipulation could not fix. After my annual checkup revealed cancer cells, I was scheduled for immediate surgery. I struggled with the irony of saying I did not care if I died and went to hell—even though I had a deep desire to go on living. I called several of my Christian friends from college days and asked for prayer.

"This is just for the surgery—not for a life change," I emphasized to Dean Hollowell when I reached her by phone.

She did not hesitate to confront the real issue. "Darlene, you know that I love you. I have continued to pray for your healing since you left the university. Jesus still loves you, and regardless of how you feel, he hasn't deserted you." She paused. "You could talk to him yourself about this operation, you know that."

"We aren't exactly on speaking terms," I murmured into the phone.

"Well, my dear, Jesus is right where you left him. He isn't the one who stopped talking or listening."

I protested. "Now, don't go preaching at me, Marie." Inside, I was glad she cared enough. "Besides, I've made some pretty big messes in my life. I'm not sure even God can fix the situations I've gotten myself into this past year." My thoughts finished the sentence. *Yeah. He can't fix my homosexuality, so how could he fix something like grand theft!*

"I will be praying for you, Darlene, but why not consider talking to him yourself? It just might help."

The surgery was successful; but even more important, I repented.

I left the gay lifestyle and confessed to grand theft, vowing to make full restitution. I sought out another church where I could find support as I worked through these issues, and also find healing. I was not only restored to my relationship with Jesus, but I was given detailed instruction in spiritual warfare.

I sought pastoral counsel and resolved that no matter how painful the process I would accept full responsibility for my past behavior. Although others had influenced me from childhood, I was the one who chose to live as a victim. I vowed to be celibate for life rather than violate the instructions of Scripture. It would be God's responsibility to heal my sexual brokenness.

I knew homosexuality was inconsistent with biblical teaching. Now I learned how to apply Scripture to times of temptation and spiritual struggle. I was determined to persist and stand firm. I was convinced that the same power that had brought healing to the Corinthian Christians was available for my healing.

Over several months, I cultivated Christian friendships to replace those friends from the gay community. I found an interdenominational Christian singles group and got involved with social activities with other people my age. I made a point of attending Bible study and church services instead of going out to the gay clubs. It was not easy. I did not always feel accepted, but I went anyway. I spent hours talking with anyone who would listen and pray with me. I was determined to find the strength to overcome the emotional bondage to my past.

I realized the sexual aspect of homosexuality was insignificant in comparison to the emotional hold that the lifestyle had created. My significance as a person and as a woman had become deeply rooted in activism and fighting for "rights." The Lord showed me that the oppression from society that I had been fighting to overcome was misplaced. There was a spiritual oppression that held my soul in bondage, and only he could free me from its grasp. My journey to wholeness had begun in earnest in 1977. The previous failures were stepping stones to a strong conviction that change was not only possible, but was available for me as I learned how to integrate the biblical truths into my daily living.

More than a decade has passed since the night when I chose to accept my responsibility for how my life turned out. The journey has not been without some rough places, and always there is the awareness that it is the grace of God that keeps me on track. I no longer struggle with the desire to return to the homosexual lifestyle. I no longer am tempted to find fulfillment and intimacy in homosexual expression. I have a new understanding of what it means to be God's woman, created in his image and equipped to behave in a sexually responsible manner. I share the same feelings as those who have never been homosexually involved, but through faith in Christ and the decision to be obedient to Scripture, I am not compelled to act out sexual feelings. I believe Scripture teaches that all sexual activity outside of marriage is sin. God has given us the special ability to draw upon his strength in this area and to live in a biblical manner.

The ministry

After I wrote about my personal journey to wholeness, *Long Road to Love* (Chosen Books), a new dimension to counseling outreach came to me. Women and men from around the country called me, wanting to talk about hope for total healing. In speaking with a real person, they were able to ask questions that books had not addressed. They were also able to hear about hundreds of others who were finding healing from sexual brokenness.

It soon became apparent that there was a need in my local area for a support group reaching out to people who struggled with their sexual orientation. After prayer and discussion with the senior pastor, I formed Paraklete Ministries—a direct outreach of Hayward Foursquare Church. Through group meetings, we offer support to anyone who desires to leave the lifestyle. We also provide counseling for families of persons with AIDS and for persons who may still be in the lifestyle and are not sure they even want to change.

This ministry to women varies somewhat from the ministry to men who want to leave the lifestyle. Men are most often into physical addiction, while women are involved in strong emotional-dependency relationships. Men are more likely to have multiple and less-committed relationships, often numbering in the hundreds. Sexual attraction for them demands a physical release that never satisfies the deep need for intimacy. Men fear growing old and not having the looks to attract a partner, yet their social interaction is geared to physical conquest, not mutual commitment.

Women have a need for intimacy and sharing. They are more likely to build a "family" environment. Sexual involvement is secondary to emotional bonding, and for this reason, lesbian relationships are more difficult to break off when one of the partners comes for counseling. Many times women do not realize they have a strong emotional dependency upon one another until one of them seeks healing.

For anyone who comes to Paraklete, we offer specific steps. The foundation stone is repentance, which is necessary for true healing. Until homosexuality is seen as a sin, and something to be forgiven, they cannot experience change. I am careful to explain that experiencing temptations to act out homosexually is not the same as choosing to act on those feelings.

When someone new attends the group, I try to learn where she is spiritually. Once we determine that she has a relationship with Jesus Christ, we establish, through Scripture, how God views homosexuality and how we can be freed from its stronghold in our lives. If she is currently in a relationship with someone, I encourage her to break off that relationship and pursue healing. I point out Scriptures on sexual responsibility and abstinence. This first step is often the most difficult for them to take.

We also offer prayer support and counseling. She is the one who must make the decision to cut off any homosexual involvement. If she has a home church, we encourage her to involve her pastoral leadership in the process of her healing. It is critical to be accountable to a minister or spiritually mature leader with whom she has regular contact. Women seem to have a knack for control and manipulation of situations, even when they desire healing from lesbianism. This is why a large part of all our ministries include an emphasis on accountability.

A woman who comes to our group must agree to have a pastor in her own church be a person to whom she is accountable. If she does not have a church family, then she must agree to have an honest accountability with a ministry leader. That person would have permission to check in with the woman and find out how she is doing during the week. The individual would also be available to pray with her on a regular basis and during times of struggle. This accountability is a vital part of ministry, and it is beneficial for dealing with the painful issues that must be worked through over a long period of time.

Along with these accountability relationships, a woman will learn to develop healthy same-sex relationships, with nonsexual involvement. This is another necessary step to sexual freedom and wholeness. We also deal with any other areas of sin she might be aware of. We encourage her to repent of all sin and past involvement in any sexual relationships. Often there are issues of alcohol or drugs she must overcome.

A statistic, which has been confirmed through other ministries as well as in my own experiences in counseling, reveals a staggering number of cases involving sexual abuse. At least 85 percent of the women I counsel have been victims of some sort of abuse. This area is not confronted and resolved with one or two prayer sessions. Many times a woman has repressed these experiences, and only the Holy Spirit can bring healing to the depths of her memory.

This is where *inner healing* and *deliverance* become involved as tools of ministry. The Lord breaks the chains of fear, guilt, and insecurity, allowing a person to overcome the woundedness of her past for the very first time. She may not even be aware it is these events that have contributed to the brokenness of her emotions in lesbian behavior. Prayer healing is the key element I have found in moving someone along the pathway of healing. Eventually there is enough confrontation that she is actually able to experience forgiveness for those who victimized her.

I have found other emotional responses, such as rejection, abandonment, and feelings of inferiority, that have created an emotional dependency setup for women struggling with lesbianism. Often a woman is trying to experience in adulthood the intimacy and nurturing that was absent in her childhood. I realized in my own life that I was trying to create in lesbian relationships the bonding I had missed with my mother.

Each of these issues is addressed in counseling and they are often new concepts for a woman to deal with. Over time, a trust is built between us that gives permission to call forth righteous behavior and response to God's Word. Initially, she may have sought understanding for why a relationship went wrong, never dreaming that God desires major reconstruction of her life, not just a Band-Aid over specific wounds.

Women who struggle with lesbianism do not all fit into the image of the militant feminist who marches for gay rights and, clad in black leather, rides a motorcycle. Some of the women are mothers or grandmothers; some have children and husbands; some are single. Many are evangelical Christians, involved in some type of ministry. All of these women share at least one common element in their struggle. They have tried to find that one person who could meet all their yearnings, and they have invested themselves emotionally in that person when they thought they had found the right person.

This is the deception of homosexuality. There is never going to be one person who will make a person whole. There is never a Ms. Right or a Mr. Right who will finally put an end to the search for filling the emptiness within. The only lasting fulfillment is in developing a love relationship with Jesus Christ.

I have learned that there are areas of spiritual bondage that need to be addressed in spiritual warfare. We minister deliverance from spiritual oppression, and we instruct these women on how to use the authority of the name of Jesus, the Word of God, and the power of the blood to wage spiritual battle with the enemy.

Weekly Bible studies are conducted to establish a consistency in biblical teaching and in how to live out the truths in our century. I also include teaching on being a new creation in Christ. Although we teach spiritual warfare, there are works of the flesh that are not demonic in nature and must be put off as an act of our will—not cast away as a demonic influence. This is practical teaching on how to live a transformed life.

Women are taught how to submit to the lordship of Jesus and gain inner support and strength from the Holy Spirit. As they learn to take personal responsibility for their actions, they find healing. Not only do they submit to the authority of their spiritual leadership, avail themselves of friendships with Christian women who are mature in their relationship with Christ and can share the principles of Scripture, but they obey God's Word no matter what the cost.

Healing for each of us comes from the transformed identity within us, which in turn expresses itself in outward behavior. There are no short cuts to wholeness, and only as the entire process is lived out will we experience lasting change. One reason I experienced so many "failures" in overcoming homosexuality is that the emphasis was always on stopping the behavior rather than healing the heart. I believe we want instant results to display as spiritual trophies. God, however, is interested in developing that loving trust that will result in permanent changes.

Temptations to sin will always be with us, but through the healing of our broken concept of sexuality, we will have strength to overcome homosexuality. Today, thousands of transformed lives declare that healing of homosexuality is not only possible, but we declare with one voice, "So if the Son sets you free, you will be free indeed"

(John 8:36, NIV). As with the Corinthians in the first century, "Such were some of us, but now, we are washed, we are cleansed, and we are made whole by the Spirit of our God!"

Chapter 2

I FOUND FREEDOM

Colin Cook

I am writing this story because I was once homosexual and now experience heterosexuality. Every turn of the path I walked is filled with signs of the gracious persistence of God.

Yet it is not easy to retrace my labyrinthine ways. To the embarrassment of my family and friends, I suffered the loss of a pastoral ministry in 1974 when my homosexuality was first exposed. Then, in 1986, because my recovery from the blinding deception and obsessiveness of homosexuality was not yet complete, I lost the homosexual-healing ministry I had built over the years. I have gotten back up again, in possession of a deeper level of healing than I have ever known and with new inner boundaries. I am back to counseling, with the sound checks and balances of supervision, church accountability, and an innovative counselor-evaluation system. So you can easily imagine that a large part of me would simply like to put the past behind me and forget it.

But I cannot, for two reasons. First, I would be selfish and disobedient to God if I kept silent for the sake of my own comfort and peace. Unless I—and others like me—confirm from personal experience that recovery and change can happen, thousands of Christians will yield to the despairing persuasion that homosexuality is an irreversible fate.

Second, I cannot recount what has happened without God's grace becoming gloriously evident. To tell my story is to say more about God than about me. God's manner of dealing with sinners is a constant astonishment. Every ounce of his being repudiates sin. Yet, in order to save me, his stubborn love overcame his repugnance toward my sinfulness. My story is therefore a recounting of *his* victory, not mine, in the midst of struggle. If my story can lead many staid and "circumcised believers" to be "astonished that the gift of the Holy Spirit has been poured out even on" homosexual "Gentiles" (cf. Acts 10:45, NIV), then the glory coming to God will make the shame coming to me worth the effort of putting this painful story into ink.

First glimmers of freedom

As a child, my defense against intimacy was a survival mechanism that God places within all emotionally wounded children. Contracting polio when I was a year old, being separated from my mother in the isolation ward of a hospital at that age for six months, and the absence of a father who was away at war for the first five years of my life left me a wounded child. After World War II ended my father returned, but though he was very caring, he was gone twenty days each month as an industrial fisherman.

At the age of eight, I realized that my disabled leg made me different from others. I particularly recall having to undress for an examination. Wearing only a shirt, and without forewarning, I was scrutinized not only by my physician but by forty male medical students. I felt humiliated by the experience and developed unconscious resentment towards others' prying eyes. I envied everyone else because they were okay—but I was not. As self-inflicted shame and fear robbed me of self-worth, I insulated my emotional life.

As I moved into puberty, my envy toward others' healthier bodies took an erotic turn, which expressed itself in homosexual fantasies. These fantasies created such powerful sexual arousals in me that I thought I needed a real homosexual intimacy. Little did I realize I was wanting men to fill the void that only God can fill, wanting them to satisfy my spiritual longings. Later, when I actually engaged in homosexual acts, I yearned to be metaphysically absorbed into the other person. For me, homosexual romanticism was my way of searching for my lost self in the person of the same sex. It was the twisted fantasy of a wounded child.

During those painful years I felt a strange abandonment, a fear and helplessness that I covered with articulate confidence. Though I knew my parents loved me, I was emotionally insulated from their love. I felt stuck in homosexual desire and believed it was impossible to be like other youth my age. Yet, I sought to get close to boys at school through emotional dominance that sometimes led to mutual masturbation. I constantly used my superior intellect to cover my deep sense of worthlessness. My hiddenness increased the intensity of my internal homosexual lust, and with it came anguish and a deepening loneliness.

And then, Christ found me when I was fifteen. I say *he* found me, because I was not even aware that I was lost or that it was him I was looking for. My boyhood fascination with flying saucers led me to what I thought was a public lecture on the subject in my home town in England. In fact, it was an evangelistic meeting on the Second Coming. From the mysterious, silent universe, whose dark skies I had gazed upon night after night and whose stillness seemed to echo the vacancy in my own soul, was to come the living, loving God. At the thought that Jesus was coming for me, I was filled with immense joy that remained in me, uninterrupted, for six months. I accepted Jesus as my Savior, gave my life over to him, and became a member of a church.

Before the first year of my conversion had come full circle, however, conflict over my sexual feelings came to a head. I went to my school friends whom I had masturbated with and asked them to forgive me. I remember the embarrassed shrugs and nods, and that was it. The bridges were burned. I was not to have another homosexual act for ten years.

But really—that was not it. Like any healthy youth, I was sexually in my prime. But every arousal, every longing, every fantasy was for men. Far from conversion solving the homosexual problem, it seemed to worsen it. For conversion created a necessary war that was to rage unabated in my soul for the next fifteen years.

Switching on

It was at Newbold College, which lies nestled in the "green belt," that great circle of countryside known as the "lungs of London," that my struggle with homosexuality took a desperate turn. I had gone there to study for the ministry. My studies brought me face to face with my deep need for holiness. Bob, Will, and I were spiritual brothers at college. We often prayed and read our Bibles together, but I never told them of the struggle deep in my troubled, aching soul.

We wanted to be holy for our God. We wanted to be like Jesus. Will and I examined as many angles as we knew to the holy life—Andrew Murray's absolute surrender, John Wesley's "second blessing," Brother Lawrence's "practice of the presence of God." For long periods I prayed half the night one day a week. Each day I prayed an hour in the morning and a half-hour in the evening. I fasted one day a week for about a year. Yet homosexuality still seemed like an impenetrable wall. Many times I wept before the Lord because of my sinful desires. "How long," my journal records, "will it be till I am made clean?"

Never was the struggle with homosexuality more vivid to me than in the attempt to develop friendships. I could not feel inwardly relaxed with men or women. To most people, I appeared to be outgoing, spiritual, and assertive. I was even voted student chaplain in my senior year. But emotionally, I was in quarantine. How could I reveal the terrifyingly real me?

I left England in 1971 to complete an M.A. degree at Andrews University in Michigan. New to the campus, I felt uncertain and lonely and far removed from the familiar climes of England. I soon heard about a class that had seminarians buzzing: Professor Hans LaRondelle's systematic theology course on righteousness by faith. LaRondelle, who had received his doctorate under the Reformed theologian G. C. Berkouwer in Holland, is a short, stocky man with a thick, Dutch accent and a subdued, mischievous joy.

The classroom was packed. Expectations were high. LaRondelle's lectures were proclamations, fit for any hour of devotion with God. From the first moment, I knew I was listening to something enormously significant to me.

There can be no renovation of man's sinful nature. . . . *Christ is the Substitute for the human race, the Propitiation.* . . . *In Christ we are treated as righteous.* . . . *We expand with joy because Christ, our Peace, makes us certain of glorification.* . . .

Condemned in the first Adam, we are justified in the Second Adam. . . . *We therefore give our bodies to his obedient service, treating them as if they were resurrected in his resurrection.* . . . *We struggle and thrash against sin* . . . *but we are freed from its power by the justifying atonement of Jesus.* . . . *Christ has triumphed over the evil powers by the Cross.* . . . *We now live in the Spirit who puts to death our carnality.*

As I walked back from class each day and sat at my desk in my little bachelor bedroom, no bigger than a one-man prison cell, my mind began to expand far beyond the cramped confines of my quarters. Thoughts sped through my brain at enormous velocity. Segments of truth, heretofore disconnected, in a flash made linkages that formed a unified whole. A switch seemed to flip on in my mind from a negative to a positive mindset. Never since my conversion had I so greatly sensed the magnificence of Jesus. Little did I realize then that I was at the beginnings of a personality reconstruction.

Christ, I could now see, had broken the powers of homosexuality in the Cross. My Jesus had been too small. It was not merely a matter of my keeping Christ in my heart. I was by the throne in him. In Jesus I was identified as whole, a heterosexual man. I had been judging myself by how I felt, not by who I was in him. God created all humankind heterosexual in Adam. Homosexuality is an illusory, false state, primarily due to the Fall and the brokenness of human relationships that ensue. It is accounted dead with Christ. My sexual lust was being stimulated by fear of abandonment and condemnation (Rom. 7:5). I had been reinforcing homosexuality for years by neurotic, whining, faithless prayer that pleads for a deliverance that is already provided.

In that little room, reality that would take years to unfold through experience was telescoped into weeks of time. The prison door was open. No matter how long it took, I knew now that I could ultimately walk free.

Yet, even this fuller revelation of the gospel did not yet break the power of homosexuality. I had learned to battle against many things by faith, but God had yet to lead me into unmitigated failure before homosexuality would yield. What God showed me about the gospel of Jesus at seminary, he was to weave into my life by means of failure over the next seventeen years. The battle was now joined, but now I saw it as a faith war, rather than a sin war.

Switching off and back on

It was during my ministry in New York City, seventeen years after my conversion, that my moral world collapsed. The motivation for wanting to be free from homosexuality was gradually, subtly shifting to a basic longing for love, a home, a family. Yet the stronger the longing, the more it appeared unreachable. The emotional isolation finally overwhelmed me. I had entered the ministry in 1965 when I was twenty-five years old. Struggling to be a friend even to myself, loneliness as a single man in the ministry stunned me. In a new city, without the security of college friends and the reassuring order of dormitory life, I closed down to everything I knew to be right and good and went out one night into the darkness and gave my body to a stranger.

I loathed what I had done. I came back to my apartment almost nauseated. In enormous distress, I poured out my soul to God in repentance. The only hope I could find in the rubble of my wickedness was that perhaps the shock of my sin might keep me from it forever.

But the repugnance faded in the memory of its brief pleasure. I sought more. Now I felt guilty and constantly feared exposure. I guarded my terrible secret during four years of ministry in England. In the impersonal life in New York City, nearly all restraints were lost. What a moral schizophrenia! Loving and serving God, preaching his Word, then proceeding to defy all he stands for as I cruised gay streets, furtively exited X-rated movie houses, or took to the illusory cocoon of gay bathhouses, only to return to my apartment, pounding with anxiety or overcome with depression.

The crisis of identity, of my "place" in the world and in God's

kingdom, was becoming gargantuan. Who was I? A lecherous wolf in
sheep's clothing, fleecing the flock, "beguiling unstable souls"? Or a
child of God with a besetting sin, trapped in the struggle described
by Paul in Romans 7, hating what I did?

Finally, after three years of ministry in New York City, attempting
to apply the gospel by faith to my homosexual struggle, I had to face
the fact of staggering defeat. I asked for a leave of absence from the
ministry because of homosexual conflict. But unknown to me, my
homosexuality had already been discovered. My conference with-
drew my ministerial license. I was devastated. And yet, it was at this
point of utter failure that my faith learned through cold-turkey
praise to grasp hold of the power of God. It was Mother Teresa, I
believe, who said, "You will never know that Jesus is all you need
until Jesus is all you've got."

He let me know that no failure and no sin, no matter how deep,
could separate me from him as long as I kept turning to him in faith
and repentance. Gradually, I learned that at the onset of temptation
I had been switching God off for fear of condemnation. I was
unaware then of what I was doing to myself spiritually—that when
the self switches God off, it switches itself off. I did not think I could
know God and sex at the same time because I had always connected
eroticism with sin and separation from God. Thus, I mistakenly
thought sin could only be overcome when sex is overcome.
Strugglers with homosexuality like myself who attempt to come
close to God will be nearly overwhelmed by their sin in the presence
of his beauty and will want to throw themselves away from him. But
with the help of God's Word and Christian supporters, I knew now
that since there is no condemnation, I could always be open to God
no matter how intense the struggle. In the ensuing years, God
brought me through enormous bondage as he restored my dominion
over sexuality through Jesus.

The Lord taught me never to ask for homosexual healing again,
but to praise him for breaking the power of homosexuality at the
Cross. Often he would encourage me not to turn my eyes away from
an attractive man (my principal way of counterfeiting Christ's
victory), but to reframe the significance of what I saw before me
through affirming what I am in Jesus and who this man is that I see
before me in the great love of God. I had to learn to experience

something of being a man among men before I could be a man among women. God has brought several heterosexual men into my life who have loved me and shown me affection with not a whiff of homosexuality. Gradually this focused faith in all that Christ can do led to the breakup of all the guilt, shame, and fear that had stimulated to much sexual sin.

When my faith stood against fantasy, erotic attraction diminished. As my homosexual behavior came under greater submission to my identity in Jesus, I sensed that I did not need what I thought I needed from homosexuality. I did not need the male physical intimacy that degenerates into sexual gratification, but Jesus showed me I needed male social intimacy that is enjoyed in conversation, work, and play. And so, homosexual behavior gradually decreased in frequency and intensity as the reality of grace filled my mind and began to remake and remold my identity. The endless search for the self in another man, the abyss of longing, was fading away.

The Lord began to awaken heterosexual desires in me. Romantic feelings for the opposite sex and the first gentle feelings of heterosexual, erotic arousal began to emerge. I learned to date women, affirming my heterosexuality and developing an entirely new awareness about myself as a man acceptable to women—a thought I had never believed possible. I also felt a new appreciation for a woman as a person. I praised God that I could see men and women through the heterosexual eyes of Jesus. I praised God for my heterosexuality when I felt most homosexual because Jesus was God's "Yes" to my heterosexuality.

In 1978 God led me to Sharon, who became my wife. I have often sensed what I believe to be the joy of God's Spirit expressing his love to me through Sharon and the pleasure of Christ's joy as he has loved Sharon through me. I realized then that homosexual healing is not an issue of trading homosexual desire for heterosexual desire, but of healing brokenness and finding wholeness, of trading lust and delusion for love through wholeness of personhood in Christ.

A hurricane passes by
Nevertheless, vestiges of homosexual behavior remained. If God had not given me first the assurance of being reckoned with Christ, I

believe my spirit would have been knocked out by the events and trials that were still to come. Instead, these trials became instruments for the completing of my heterosexuality. The loss of Quest Learning Center, a homosexual healing ministry I had founded, came about because of my homosexual behavior, which involved some of my counselees.

Despite experiencing heterosexual love, I was still blinded to its greater component, that of loyalty to my wife. I had rationalized certain behaviors for years, like an alcoholic trying to swap beer for the hard stuff. Some behaviors, I told myself, like prolonged holding and hugging and massages without clothes, were not sexual because they were not genital—even though they were arousing. I told myself they helped me and others to desensitize sexual feelings or fulfill child-parent needs long neglected. I now look back in amazement that I actually believed these lies, having denied that an erotic, nongenital massage was disloyal to Sharon.

I could not, or rather would not, see that a massage charged with sexual energy, even though not sexually consumated, was treachery to the tender intimacy of our marriage. I was afraid to confess these sins to my wife or reach out for help. But they affected the spontaneity of our marital intimacy. Fear blocked the ease to sexual loving. I forgot that loyalty to my spouse and keeping myself pure and only for her is true personhood and a heterosexuality far beyond the mere ability to respond sexually.

And then, my secrecy burst wide open. My dishonesty and sin were exposed. God shook me awake through Christian friends and forced me to face him, myself, and others. I saw that while there is a legitimate desensitizing and reparenting in the healing of homosexuality, mine was mixed with seduction. I was shocked at the level of my denial and at the hurt I had brought upon trusting friends and vulnerable counselees. My reputation, mind games, and lewd distractions were seen for the pathetic little heap they were when Jehovah the Hurricane passed by.

The confession of my sins deeply wounded Sharon—so much so that I wondered whether it would have been better to have remained silent. Her initial reaction of pain and withdrawal taught me how precious and loyal her love had been to me, and yet how delicate. Since then, I have often recoiled at the cruelty of my unfaithfulness, leading me to greater sensitivity. The Lord "strikes and heals," or perhaps more accurately, "heals as he strikes" (Isa. 19:22, NEB).

My sexual compulsions—and a crippling homosexual romanticism—through God's glorious and severe mercy finally disappeared in September 1986. The fantasies had shifted first from being a compulsion, to becoming a pleasant diversion, to becoming, finally, something I did not want, because the false need for them had gone and I could say good-bye to them. Sometimes the fight of faith seemed nearly to tear me apart as the only "self" I had ever known was pushed aside and my true self was allowed to emerge. But a bruised reed Jesus will not break. I have come to know that God can do what he promises.

Never have I had such a profound respect for trials. They led us to Christ and to the healing of our marriage. Sharon is a courageous woman, a woman of faith who has forgiven me in Jesus. That we are fully committed to each other and our children is the deepest satisfaction of my life—next to the Lord himself. It is with her, more than anyone else, that I have known the call to love and the sharing of our image of God as one. I am glad Scripture says that a man and a woman shall *become* one—that there is a growing into oneness. I often had fears that Sharon would not love me when she knew me at my deepest levels. Thus, I have had to learn to resist the tendency to want to withdraw, not to be known. Through Sharon's help I have learned to tell her who I am. We have found that the fear behind the revelation of ourselves begins to dissipate as soon as it is shared. To receive each others' calm reaction to uncomfortable disclosures makes us seem more normal to each other.

I have always been amazed to discover how this opening of the window on each other creates the desire for closeness. If Sharon or I shut each other out for long, we become bored with each other, irritable, and alien. But to share our feelings with each other—even if they are negative ones—breaks down the detachment. The boredom disappears, the feeling of missing each other returns, tenderness comes back, as well as the interest in the little things about each other, including the interest in sex.

As my faith grabbed the truth I had learned and imposed it upon all my homosexual feelings, I came to experience viscerally that the "I" that is crucified with Christ and now lives by faith in the Son of

God is not the "I" of homosexuality. Personhood and homosexuality are not the same. They are like two circles, the one (homosexuality) superimposed on the other (personhood) so that they are confused as one. Slowly those two circles pulled apart, the homosexual circle diminishing in size over the years, its steely bonds gradually disintegrating into powder, drifting away before the gentle, invincible wind of God's Spirit.

Despite my stumbling, God did not let go of me. By his grace and the love and courage of my wife, I now stand free: blissfully, gratefully free. And what is more beautiful still, I am not so much free *from* something as I am free *for* something: free to enjoy the love of my children, free to walk as one with my wife through our orchard, free to feel alive and to redirect energy, previously wasted, into ways of leading others to the same joyful freedom I have come to know.

Chapter 3

THE EXODUS STORY: THE GROWTH OF EX-GAY MINISTRY

Bob Davies

*Exodus International is a worldwide coalition of Christian outreaches
to men and women seeking to overcome homosexuality through the
power of Jesus Christ. In this chapter, Exodus's executive director
shares his perspective on the development of this worldwide outreach.*

When God first gave me a glimpse of my future ministry
with homosexuals, I was horrified.

It was an early summer day in 1976, and I had been praying about
my future for weeks. My six-month evangelism schooling at Youth
With A Mission's outreach center in southern Germany was ending.
What did God have in store for me next?

I was outside working—pulling weeds from between the cobblestones on the driveway—when a very clear picture came into my mind: I was back home in Vancouver, British Columbia, Canada, standing outside a well-known gay bar, handing out tracts to homosexual men going in and out the front door.

An evangelistic ministry to homosexuals? You've got to be kidding, I thought. *Lord, I'll do* anything *but that!*

The idea of such a ministry terrified me—not because I was afraid of gays. On the contrary, I understood them very well. For years, I also struggled with homosexual feelings. Although I had never acted on them, same-sex attractions caused me deep guilt and shame. I was determined that no one would ever discover that part of me.

Later, back home in Canada, I saw a book called *Gay Liberation* in a local Christian bookstore. Written by a woman only identified as "Roberta," she revealed her life as a lesbian and how God had freed her from that lifestyle. Having never read such a book before, I promptly sent a letter to the author by way of her publisher, confessing some of my own homosexual tendencies and struggles.

She wrote back, telling me how she had started a small outreach to homosexuals and asking if I could help her put together a cassette tape of testimonies. "I believe you could be a very important part of this ministry," she said. "We could do it together." I responded by explaining that I wasn't interested in ministering to homosexuals.

I had no idea that Roberta Laurila had been praying for me—and for hundreds of others like me who would eventually be raised up around the world to work in the field of ex-gay ministry.

The beginning

December 1967, Grand Rapids—Nine years before I picked up Roberta's book, she had taken several sleeping pills. It was two weeks before Christmas, and she was severely depressed. At 2:00 A.M., she was still awake; then the spiritual vision came.

In her mind's eye, Roberta saw a series of large signs, like the billboards on Highway 131 south of her home city of Grand Rapids. As the signs flashed by, she read on each one the name of a different country, many of them in Europe. As the image changed, Roberta found herself moving down a hallway, looking into a series of small rooms. In each room were people talking on phones, counseling individuals in distress. She sensed that many people were being led to the Lord. The vision switched again. Roberta peered down into a huge stadium where an evangelist was speaking. After the invitation was given, hundreds of homosexuals came forward seeking salvation.

Roberta sensed the Lord's presence in her small bedroom. Her spirit discerned the message of the three scenes from the vision: One day there would be a worldwide network of ministries to help homosexuals come out of that lifestyle. She also sensed God speaking to her: "If you'll leave your situation, I'll use you mightily." Roberta was living with her lover, but three weeks later she left.

Because of her burden to see homosexuals set free, she prayed daily for God to raise up counselors throughout the world. Her prayers were finally answered in the early and mid-1970s. Christian outreaches to homosexuals were started in such diverse places as Los Angeles, New York City, Minneapolis, and San Francisco, as well as in foreign countries: England, Holland, South Africa, and Australia.

As men and women were leaving the gay life, they gave their friends a startling message: There *is* a way out of homosexuality!

An early pioneer
May 1973, San Rafael—One of the first ex-gay ministries was founded in 1973 in the San Francisco Bay Area. Love In Action began when God dramatically intervened in the life of a highly successful businessman named Frank Worthen.

On May 24, 1973, Frank had locked his office door and was walking toward the back entrance of his import store, car keys in hand. He intended to drive fifteen miles south into San Francisco and visit a new homosexual hangout that had just opened. Suddenly, Frank's mind flashed back to the time of his father's death when he was fourteen. "God, please be my Father for the rest of my life," he had prayed. Frank had committed his life to the Lord as a teenager, but he had subsequently left the church to pursue homosexual activities. Despite his life of immorality, however, he felt that the Lord had been watching over him.

Frank now sensed God's ultimatum: *If you continue in rebellion, I will remove my hand of protection from your life.*

After pausing in the hallway, Frank turned to one of his Christian employees. "Michael," he asked, "can you take me to your church right now?"

After they drove to a little chapel several miles away, Frank and his young employee knelt in front of an altar. Frank wept, confessing his sins. Over the next twenty minutes, he sensed a growing release from twenty-five years of rebellion.

Frank began attending church several times a week with his young employee from work. Despite his homosexual background, men and women in the small fellowship embraced him warmly and soon formed a tight web of support around him. "They visited me during the week and asked how I was doing," recalls Frank. Many of them shopped at his popular import store, never failing to offer encouragement to the newest member of their church. Frank admits that his survival as a Christian depended on the emotional and prayer support he received in those early days.

"I was forty-four by this time, and sex was increasingly hard to come by," he says. "Yet, after my recommitment to Christ, young men who had ignored me became sexually available to me. Satan brought all sorts of tempting situations to me. One night I picked up a hitchhiker, a fine-looking young man, who let me know he was interested in going home with me. But I witnessed to him about Christ. I couldn't believe I was actually saying no to his overtures. The Lord was strengthening me."

Although there were times when Frank was severely tempted, he never once fell back into his old immoral lifestyle. It soon became apparent that the Lord had his hand on Frank in a special way. Within a week of his conversion, other Christians came to him—men and women who were seeking to overcome homosexuality. Six months later he recorded his testimony on a cassette tape and advertised it in a local underground paper, *The Berkeley Barb*. During the first year, over sixty men wrote for the tape.

Two years later, six men and women involved in Frank's growing ministry had their stories published in a book called *The Third Sex?* Letters begging for help poured in from around the world. Since the ministry demanded so much time, Frank sold his business and launched into full-time Christian outreach.

Frank still thought his ministry was unique in 1975. To his knowledge, he was the only Christian who had ever come out of the gay lifestyle and started an outreach to other homosexuals. But that was soon to change in a dramatic way.

The summit conference

September 1976, Los Angeles—Frank Worthen was sitting at a table with Barbara Johnson, who had discovered the previous summer that her youngest son was involved in the homosexual lifestyle. Devastated, she had gone to Melodyland Hotline Center for counseling, then contacted Frank after reading *The Third Sex?*

"Your ministry isn't the only outreach to homosexuals," she informed him. "Did you know there's a similar ministry in Anaheim?" Frank was so excited that he flew to Southern California to meet the staff of EXIT, the "Ex-gay Intervention Team," at Melodyland. That afternoon, Frank and the EXIT staff decided to convene a weekend seminar for anyone else around the country who was involved in helping homosexuals find freedom.

After inquiring about other ex-gay ministries and sending invitations to over a dozen groups throughout the country, sixty-two delegates gathered at Melodyland for a three-day weekend conference in September of 1976. The air sparkled with excitement from the opening session. "The atmosphere was electric," said one woman. Everyone sensed that God was doing something special.

Until that weekend, ex-gay ministries had felt isolated because they were largely unsupported by the church at large. Many Christians were too embarrassed to discuss heterosexual issues, let alone homosexuality. The "gay world" was still hidden, mysterious, threatening. Openly testifying of deliverance from such an abhorrent lifestyle was taboo. As one person said, "You can talk about overcoming drugs, alcohol—even adultery or murder. But don't talk about being gay." Some Christians also had other irrational fears, such as the fear of their children being seduced by former homosexuals in their church. Consequently, ex-gay ministries received little financial and emotional support from the rest of the church.

But now, for the first time, a roomful of people sensed their common calling from God: helping men and women find freedom from homosexuality. This gathering was later dubbed the "EXIT Summit Conference" and became an annual event, with attendance increasing tenfold in the years ahead.

One woman who attended the first conference was Robbi Kenney, a friend of Roberta Laurila. During the final session, delegates discussed one important issue: Where do we go from here? After approving the idea of ministries loosely affiliated with one another, they deliberated on what to call this fledgling work. "How about the name 'Exodus'?" suggested Robbi. "Homosexuals finding freedom reminds me of the children of Israel leaving the bondage of Egypt and moving towards the Promised Land." After they unanimously accepted Robbi's suggestion, the name "Exodus" was born.

Before leaving the gathering, they also adopted a statement of intent: "EXODUS is an international Christian effort to reach homosexuals and lesbians. EXODUS upholds God's standard of righteousness and holiness, which declares that homosexuality is sin, and affirms his love and redemptive power to recreate the individual. It is the goal of EXODUS International to communicate this message to the Church, to the gay community, and to society."

The opposition begins
June 1977, Oakland—During the following year, Exodus ministries flourished in a euphoria of youthful zeal. The second conference, held in Oakland, California, in June of 1977, attracted over one hundred eager participants.

Opposition began in earnest with reporters from local gay and secular newspapers invading the opening session of the conference. The *San Francisco Examiner* branded Exodus a "fundamentalist, anti-gay organization that uses deprogramming techniques." The local gay press lamented, "Many of the people present were pathetic messes." Most of the media linked Exodus with the Anita Bryant Crusade that was making national headlines at the time.

Unfortunately, numerous ministries did not survive the next two years. The reasons were varied. Outreaches that had begun in isolation from the body of Christ were particularly vulnerable. Without proper spiritual and emotional support, leaders became discouraged and quit. In some cases, the naïveté of a local church contributed to a ministry's demise. A few churches enthusiastically endorsed the idea of ex-gay ministry but showed a serious lack of judgment in choosing a director for their outreach. Having "a testimony" was seen as the only qualification necessary, even if an ex-gay leader had only been a Christian for several months.

Some people featured in national Christian magazines had a moral relapse soon after their stories were published. Sadly enough, most of these catastrophes could have been avoided. People's stories were often written prematurely. Back then, ex-gay testimonies were unique; publishers did not examine how long these people had been out of their homosexual behavior before pushing them before the public eye.

The early days of the ex-gay movement were similar to the early days of aviation: Some pioneers soared to new and unknown heights, but others experienced spectacular and highly publicized crashes. A few churches, and even whole denominations, were so burned that it took them years to consider once again a healing ministry for homosexuals.

Spiritual warfare also was evident. The homosexual world was Satan's domain, and until that time, few Christians had publicly testified to a homosexual past. Indeed, many churches were dubious as to whether such a change was even possible. The enemy wanted to hide the possibility of healing. Those who came forward with such claims were hit with increased temptations.

The ex-gay movement also attracted ridicule from various religious progay groups. One leader of a national progay ministry published booklets "exposing" the Exodus movement, particularly spotlighting any ex-gay leader who fell back into sin.

Exodus leaders also faced opposition at the local level. One ministry director, speaking at a local Presbyterian seminary, encountered faculty members who stood up during an evening presentation and openly ridiculed his position. Other ministries found it nearly impossible to get bookings in local churches because of their subject matter.

The press, the church, and spiritual warfare—all provided a challenge to the ex-gay movement. But perhaps the most difficult test was just ahead: internal strife within Exodus itself.

Friction from within

June 1979, San Rafael—It was a sunny Sunday morning. I couldn't wait to get to church. Frank Worthen was due back from the annual Exodus conference, and I was anxious to hear all the details. I spotted Frank almost as soon as I walked into church. "How was the conference?" I asked eagerly. Frank looked past me. "I don't even want to talk about it," he muttered and walked away.

I was stunned.

Having recently relocated from Vancouver, I had been at Love In Action for only three weeks. In the following months, I overheard bits and pieces about what had transpired at the Exodus IV conference. What I heard was not encouraging. The gathering, held at a retreat center near Johnstown, Pennsylvania, had been a fiasco. Only ex-gay ministry leaders were invited, and the week was anticipated as a time of intense prayer and seeking the Lord about unresolved questions related to overcoming homosexuality.

As the week progressed, however, a crisis developed. It soon became apparent that there were two groups of people at the conference, both with a very different opinion on a crucial issue. One group insisted that the term *ex-gay* implied heterosexuality and the possibility of marriage; another group thought that sexual orientation could not be changed, and they were ready to settle for "homosexual celibacy."

Each side was adamant, with tempers flaring, harsh words said, and feelings hurt. Disunity engulfed the group. Discouragement was rife. By the end of the week, there was one main question on the minds of many leaders: Would Exodus survive?

These controversies actually were not new. Brewing under the surface since the inception of Exodus, they came to a full boil the week of Exodus IV in 1979. But they had been prodded along by a speaker at the previous year's conference. "Our acceptance of gay people, both orientation and behavior, must be greater," he told delegates. "God may never enable me to lose my gay orientation, no matter how hard I try. But I'm glad that I'm still part of a body of believers who will take me as I am."

The speaker's suggestion that his same-sex orientation might never change startled Exodus board members, who immediately held an impromptu meeting in the hallway outside the classroom. They decided to finish the session with a discussion with the entire group. "It sounds like you're offering no way out," a ministry leader challenged the speaker. By the time other opinions were expressed, it was clear that a Pandora's box of controversy had been opened.

This controversy was not easily resolved for several reasons. The ex-gay movement was still young, and some ministry directors were not yet solidly grounded in the Scriptures. A lot of their opinions were based on personal experience—and they were still in the process of being healed of their homosexual past. When it came to answering questions on the nature of redemption and sanctification—specifically applied to the homosexual issue—few of these leaders were sufficiently informed to offer in-depth answers. It was becoming increasingly obvious that there was a variety of opinions within Exodus on the fundamental question: "What does it really mean to be healed from homosexuality?"

New understanding

1979–1980, San Rafael—In July of 1979, a new series of teachings began appearing monthly in the *Outpost* newsletter, an ex-gay ministry in Minneapolis. Written by Ed Hurst, the material presented a startling new truth to me: Homosexuality was just the surface symptom of deeper "root" issues that needed healing.

Over the next year, Ed covered such topics as self-pity, rejection, fear, envy, deception, rebellion, and bitterness. He related them all to the specific issue of homosexuality. "If I could just get rid of this one problem [homosexuality] in my life, then I'd really have it together as a Christian" had always been my attitude. Now, for the first time, I recognized how extensive a healing God needed to do in my life. Just as poison applied to the roots of a tree eventually brings the whole structure crashing down, so I had to allow the Lord to deal with the hidden "roots" of my struggles with my sexual identity.

In one sense, the "tap root" of my struggle had ended when I said "yes" to the Lord by moving to Love In Action. At that time, I had handed over my sexuality to him in a new way, extending his lordship into that area of my life. I've come to realize that the lordship of Christ can be an ongoing decision, as God brings new areas of our life to light, areas that still need to be surrendered to him.

In the ministry, I saw the importance of "walking in the light" with other believers, being willing to open the deepest parts of my life to those who could offer loving support. Because I had never acted on my homosexual desires, I did not have to struggle with such issues as achieving celibacy or leaving a lover. But the "roots" that prompted the same-sex attractions were just as deep in me as in others who came to Love In Action seeking help.

In fact, I discovered that after others had been at the ministry for some months, or even several years, they came to the same point where I had begun when I first arrived: dealing with the deeper issues or "roots." As they practiced sexual purity, they no longer worried about sexual involvement with another person; instead, they wrestled with such issues as pornography, masturbation, and a disciplined thought life. As the healing process continued, deeper and deeper levels of one's life were touched. Freedom was a process, occurring step by step over a period of time.

I also came to appreciate the church's role in healing. My home church in San Rafael was a perfect example. Church of the Open Door is an interdenominational fellowship that is very open to the ministry of Love In Action, which has been intimately involved in the church for over fifteen years. During a typical Sunday morning service, up to half the people leading the service are graduates of the LIA program—from organist to pianist to soloist to sound technician. Members are involved in the church structure at every level.

In this church, I experienced something new: honest communication and fellowship with men who had never been gay. In previous churches, I had socialized well in singles' groups, but I had always carefully hidden my sexual struggles. At Open Door, such anonymity was impossible—but more important, it did not matter.

Men in the church were friendly and affectionate to all of us Love In Action members. Their support was very affirming. I also learned about the struggles of nongays. I was amazed at their private confessions: Straight men would tell me that they, too, had struggled with the homosexual issue in some way in their past, although not to the same depth I had. They may have experienced a certain curiosity, or had an experience with another boy during early adolescence, or had some doubt or question about their own sexual identity somewhere along the line. Some had also struggled with pornography and/or masturbation. Sexual purity was an issue for *all* of us.

My relationships took on a whole new depth that I had never experienced before. For years, I had lived behind walls of fear and isolation, keeping the truth of my homosexual struggles carefully hidden. Now I was living "outside the walls" for the first time in my life. And in ways I did not even know at the time, I was being healed at a deeper level of my identity as a male than I had ever known.

Outside input

June 1980, Seattle—By June of 1980, the uproar from Exodus IV had subsided and the next conference was a resounding success. Keynote speaker for the week was Arthur Katz, a Messianic Jew with a prophetic ministry, who presented a challenging call to personal holiness to the fifty-one conferees. Katz's message was "something a lot of us needed," recalls Robbi Kenney, a member of the Exodus board during that time. "Art was instrumental in bringing some new understanding of what God was requiring of us all in the area of personal holiness."

At one memorable session, Katz told delegates about the first time his Christian community in rural Minnesota had to slaughter a pig, which had put up a horrible fight before it died. "That's what the sin nature is like," he told us. "It kicks and squirms and squeals until it's totally dead." Katz explained that our sinful past also fights to survive, but we have to put it to death daily through the power of Christ working in us. His story was a graphic illustration not soon forgotten.

Exodus leaders realized an important lesson: The church at large has important input to offer our small group of ex-gay members. Any group in isolation can head off into a doctrinal wasteland, but with the help of the whole body of Christ, Exodus can stay on track.

Arthur Katz made another significant contribution to Exodus that week. With his prodding, the board took an unequivocal stand against the idea that a homosexual orientation was somehow acceptable or even neutral. The general consensus among Exodus leaders from that point on: Temptation is not sin (Heb. 4:15), but the homosexual orientation is an expression of humanity's sinfulness and cannot coexist with a total commitment to Jesus Christ. That same year, the Exodus policy statement on homosexuality was published. Drawn up by several members of the Exodus board, it took a firm stand: "Liberation from homosexuality includes repentance from homosexual behavior, identity and lifestyle."

Frank Worthen left no doubt where he stood when his ministry, Love In Action, published a newsletter that September: "At a recent conference, I took issue with some brothers who were calling themselves 'homosexual Christians.' In our discussion, which lasted several hours, I used the word 'anathema' to describe how I regarded the use of the term. . . . I utterly reject the joining of two words that are so diametrically opposed to one another."

Frank said this position denied one of the major themes of the New Testament: "We have a new identity in Christ." A few people quietly left Exodus at this point, but most stayed and embraced this position.

Increased visibility

January 1983, Denver—"Exodus has tended to be an inward-looking group," said Alan Medinger to the rest of the Exodus board during their midwinter meeting in Denver. "Our vision has been too narrow. We've not been on the offensive in proclaiming Christ's power to deliver people from homosexuality."

The other board members agreed with Alan's challenge and decided to relocate the Exodus office permanently in San Rafael, California. Public exposure for the annual conference was increased. Exodus VIII that year was advertised in several national publications. An overseeing board of reference was established, drawing well-known people who could "watch over" the board of directors. This ten-person board of reference consisted of Christian leaders from numerous denominations.

Increasing publicity came to Exodus ministries during the next several years. National publications such as *Charisma* and *Christianity Today* reported on our activities, prompting a flood of mail to the San Rafael office. These magazines affirmed the legitimacy of the Exodus movement. For example, Beth Spring wrote the following statements in the September 21, 1984, issue of *Christianity Today*: "Until more churches learn to address the acute spiritual and emotional needs of homosexuals, groups that are part of the Exodus coalition intend to fill the gap. Staffed by people who have endured the pain of passage out of homosexual behavior, these ministries offer authentic models of change for men and women still struggling with a misplaced sexual identity."

A new urgency

June 1987, St. Paul—"We are in a spiritual battle of staggering proportions," said Alan Medinger in his closing address at the Exodus XII conference. Over two hundred men and women from forty-five different ex-gay ministries around the nation listened attentively as Alan continued: "Until now, widespread church support for redemptive ministry to homosexuals has been lacking, but AIDS is changing that. Voices in the church previously speaking out in defense of the homosexual lifestyle are now strangely silent."

During the early 1980s, Exodus ministries had noticed a growing disinterest in the church over the issue of homosexuality. Multiple books on the subject had poured off the evangelical presses in the late 1970s. Silence followed, however. The theology of homosexual behavior had been fervently debated in mainline denominations, but most of their committees subsequently turned their attention to other "urgent" issues of the day.

Then came AIDS.

Suddenly, the topic of homosexuality was of crucial concern again. Pastors around the nation were shocked to discover that members of their churches had been infected with the AIDS virus, mostly through homosexual activities. The problem of homosexuality—even within evangelical churches—could no longer be ignored. The AIDS issue created a new wave of interest in ex-gay ministry.

Numerous ex-gay ministries formed, most of them seeking affiliation with Exodus. Drawing on the lessons of the past, the Exodus board listed strict qualifications for these new ministries desiring Exodus endorsement. The most important qualification concerned local accountability. In the early days, too many ministries had operated as "lone rangers," without any supervision from their immediate church community. Exodus ministries now were required to be accountable to a local pastor or church board.

Exodus leaders were also cautious about endorsing ministries begun by new converts. Therefore, ministry directors were required to be free from homosexual activity for at least one year before their application for endorsement would be considered. All ministry directors were also required to be active participants in a local church, so that Exodus leaders would be thoroughly integrated into their congregations.

These changes in ministry standards during the mid-1980s produced increased stability and maturity in the ex-gay movement. The recidivism rate among ministry leaders declined drastically compared to the early days of Exodus. As ministry directors matured, an increasing number entered into marriage and parenthood. These men and women became leaders in their local church fellowships *apart from* their homosexual background—rather than their "testimony" forming the basis of leadership.

The Exodus conferences attracted an increasing number of pastors and lay counselors who did not have a homosexual past but realized the urgent need of addressing the homosexual issue in their local community. Outstanding pastors, denominational leaders, psychologists, and other Christian leaders spoke at the annual conferences, which grew to include over four hundred participants. Theological imbalances were hammered out as these speakers addressed many issues from a wide spectrum of denominational viewpoints.

International growth

Exodus also saw a significant growth internationally during the early 1980s. Five participants came to the 1981 Exodus conference from the Netherlands. One of them, Johan van de Sluis, had been out of homosexuality for over ten years and was directing a street ministry in Amsterdam. After returning from the conference, he helped launch a European coalition of ex-gay ministries. He wrote letters to many Christian organizations in Europe, and the response was so positive that Johan convened a European Exodus conference.

In May of 1982, about seventy-five men and women gathered at "De Burght," a Christian conference center on the south coast of Holland. Participants came from the Netherlands, Great Britain, West Germany, Denmark, France, Switzerland, and the United States. After expressing a desire to be an autonomous group with their own board, Exodus Europe was off and running.

Meanwhile, similar activities were occurring in the South Pacific. Peter Lane, a former worker for Teen Challenge in Queensland, Australia, had been street witnessing to homosexuals for over six years when he visited Love In Action in San Rafael during the summer of 1983. He returned home with a new determination to help develop ex-gay ministries throughout Australia and New Zealand. During the next five years, several ministries began or were strengthened through Peter's enthusiastic support. Interestingly, most were directed by men who, like Peter, had never struggled with the homosexual issue in their own lives. The resulting coalition joined the growing international network as "Exodus South Pacific" in January 1988. Ministries in Australia and New Zealand now gather for their own annual conference.

Exodus International currently encompasses seventy ministries in forty different U.S. states, two Canadian outreaches, ten ministries in six European countries, seven ministries in Australia, and three in New Zealand. Plans are also under way for ex-gay ministries to be established in other world regions, primarily South America and the Far East. An increasing number of North American workers are being sent overseas to establish new works or to strengthen already-existing foreign outreaches.

No one is more thrilled about the growth of Exodus than Roberta Laurila, whose prayers through the years have continued unabated since her vision back in 1967.

"Much has happened since that time," she agrees. "Answering my prayers, God has called forth former gays to minister, and I have been blessed beyond measure. What a wonderful God he is!"

All around the world, former homosexuals share her excitement about a life-changing God. And they are grateful for the prayers of one faithful woman who led the way.

Chapter 4

COMING OUT

Tim Stafford

Over fifteen years ago, I started a column on love and sex for *Campus Life*, a Christian youth magazine. Among the letters I received was a steady stream from young people who felt sexually attracted to their own gender. Nobody could express more fear and despair. They wanted to be Christians yet feared they were damned. Could anything remove this curse of homosexuality?

Christians who believe the Bible condemns homosexual acts have had two options to offer such people: celibacy and a changed sexual orientation. But is the second option really possible? Many homosexuals have gone through years of wanting to change, praying for change. Some have undergone extensive therapy, and some have married, hoping they will "snap out of it." Yet many therapists and sex researchers view change as impossible.

For years, however, small Christian groups and individual Christians have made claims about their changed orientation. These groups have tended to appear and disappear, sometimes when their leaders have retreated into a gay lifestyle. Nonetheless, "ex-gay" Christian groups have survived, and many seem to be growing.

I set out to know some of the leaders of the ex-gay movement, to probe their stories and to ask questions about their techniques. They offer hope to desperate people; is the hope realistic? I brought some skepticism to the task. The ex-gay movement has trenchant critics, and the failures of some ex-gay leaders have been widely publicized. I have been a Christian and a journalist long enough to know that Christians sometimes make claims (about healings, about conversions, about finances) that don't pan out. In sexuality, particularly, things are not always what they seem.

Leading the exodus
Exodus International is an umbrella organization for about fifty ministries devoted to helping homosexuals change. Scattered across the country, they are nearly all one-person shows. Small as it is, Exodus is the primary force in ex-gay ministry. I learned that its executive board would be meeting in Mendocino, on the wild, sparsely inhabited north coast of California. I was invited to visit.

After a long, misty drive, I pulled into the Lord's Land, a hippie colony from the sixties turned into a Christian retreat center. It looked it. But despite the variety of weirdly shaped cottages dotting the landscape, inside the largest house I found a pleasant and stimulating group of people:

• Sy Rogers, who had his first homosexual encounter when he was eight years old. After college he entered a sex-change program at Johns Hopkins. He spent one-and-a-half years taking sex hormones and learning to "pass" as a woman in preparation for the surgery. Shortly before the operation, however, Johns Hopkins's sex-change program was canceled. In desperation, Sy cried out to God. That was ten years ago. He now has been married for seven years and is the father of a three-year-old child. In an effort to reach out to others, he has begun an ex-gay ministry in Orlando, Florida.

• Alan Medinger, who had practiced a double life for ten years. While married with children, he secretly cruised gay hangouts. At the time of his conversion some fifteen years ago, he ended all homosexual behavior. He says, "I fell in love with my wife in a way I had never thought possible." Medinger says he has not been seriously tempted in ten years.

● Luanna Hutchison, who, from an early age, had it fixed in her mind "that daddies wanted sons." She says, "I was determined to be the best son my daddy could want." In college she became involved in a lesbian relationship. Eventually she contacted an Exodus ministry, and a process of healing began.

● Frank Worthen, who as a teenager was introduced to homosexuality by his pastor. He moved to San Francisco at nineteen and lived an active gay life for twenty-five years. A successful businessman, Worthen felt increasingly depressed by the life he was living. Then he was converted through one of his employees. The founder of Exodus, Worthen was celibate for twelve years and has now been married for four.

● Andy Comiskey, who joined the Southern Californian gay scene as a high-school student. After four years he began a "slow but sure transition to a new life." He has now been married for eight years and has four children.

● Bob Davies, who grew up with homosexual feelings but, becoming a Christian at age twelve, never acted them out. While training to be a missionary ten years ago, he realized that he needed first to resolve his sexual identity. He contacted an Exodus ministry for help. Four years ago he was married.

● Frank Rogers is a middle-aged man whose son's gay lifestyle led him to launch an ex-gay ministry.

● Starla Allen, who was raped by a family friend at the age of thirteen and subsequently longed to be tough and invulnerable. In college she began a five-year sexual relationship with another woman. A friend led her to the Lord, and she began to change.

A young movement
The nine of us sat around a table and talked most of the day. Ex-gay groups are accused of being deeply homophobic, but I certainly did not seem to be dealing with a group of gay bashers. They did not paint lurid pictures of their past, nor of the gay community. They emphasized the loneliness, the sense of hopelessness and futility.

They were not entirely fond of the way their testimonies are sometimes transmitted in the press, suggesting overnight conversions to heterosexuality. They were describing gradual change, with its roots in ordinary Christian discipleship.

I was interested in this emphasis on gradual healing, particularly since I knew that most Exodus ministries are in the charismatic stream of the church. In fact, one prominent charismatic leader had told me that homosexuality was caused by a demon; that when this demon is cast out the problem of homosexuality ends. But these ex-gay leaders all disavowed this. Evil spirits affected some people's lives, they said, but they did not see deliverance (exorcism) as key to their ministries. They did not seem to have any exotic techniques; most of what they did sounded similar to other evangelical ministries—except for the specific problems they deal with.

Did they have any scientific studies that would corroborate their claims? They said they did not. They emphasized how young their movement is—just over ten years old—and that their members had no time, money, or expertise to do a professional study. Some studies were beginning, and they hoped these would show the realism of what they were attempting.

When I asked about a cure rate, however, I could feel the discomfort level rise. Only with prodding would they give estimates—from 50 to 90 percent. If people were truly being changed, I thought, why not talk about statistics? But then someone asked what the general "cure rate" for the church was. How many Christians really overcome the patterns they have grown up with—patterns of pride, or fear, or arrogance? Even with the highly committed, the "cure rate" would be difficult to pin down.

As we talked, it became clear that they did not think of homosexuality as a disease of the body with absolutely definable symptoms. They did not "cure" it as one would cure measles. They thought of homosexuality more as a disease of the soul. For the most part, such things can only be changed gradually, only incrementally.

The Exodus leaders all say they never chose to be homosexual; from their earliest memories they felt different. They believe that while each case is unique, homosexuality can usually be traced to a deficient relationship between a child and a father. (They rely heavily on the work of psychologist Elizabeth Moberly.) Their classic cases are those in which the father was physically absent or emotionally detached. (For women, they say, sexual abuse is often a strong factor as well.) The result can be basic gender confusion—a lack of certainty as to one's own well-being as a member of one's sex, and a longing to be accepted and loved by one's own sex. This longing is legitimate, they believe, but can be eroticized at puberty and never really resolved. Gay experiences, they said, never solve this basic sense of loss.

Only once that day did I sense self-consciousness: when the subject swung to marriage. All of the men were married, and one of the women said she was in love. Yet marriage was not the unnoted, taken-for-granted reality it is in most Christian gatherings. It was not that they regarded marriage as "proof" that change was real. They admitted that homosexuals sometimes try to cure themselves through marriage, and they recognized the potential tragedy in that. Marriage was important to them, I gathered, because it was so far beyond what any of them had expected.

A Philadelphia story
I was impressed by what I had seen and heard at the Exodus board meeting. Just the personal stories were impressive. But there was something more. This fact would strike me repeatedly as I carried on many interviews. People in ex-gay ministries seemed comfortable with themselves. They indulged in good-humored banter; they did not seem like people trying to convince themselves.

To examine ex-gay ministries more closely, however, I would need to talk at length with individuals, and I would need to talk to critics. A trip to Philadelphia took me to Harvest Ministries, which rents a spacious but time-worn second floor in a downtown building. John Freeman was the only paid employee, and he showed me around the office. There was not much to show: plenty of space and not much to fill it. Much of the work there is done through individual counseling; in addition, a weekly support group had attracted twenty-five to thirty men all summer. Harvest hoped to add another staff member for ministry to AIDS patients. (They have since done so, along with two part-time staff.)

Harvest is one of the few Exodus ministries that comes from a noncharismatic base. Freeman graduated from Westminster Theological Seminary, and Harvest was started under the wing of James Boice's Tenth Presbyterian Church.

Freeman grew up in Chattanooga, Tennessee. "My father was only partly there," he said, "and not really very much there when he was." From his earliest memories, Freeman remembers not fitting in with other males. He had "typical" adolescent sexual experiences with other males, but "the others outgrew it. Mine wasn't just a stage." He continued furtively acting out his homosexuality until he was twenty-one.

Then, while working for the postal service, Freeman met a Christian couple who "adopted" him. They invited him to attend their church. He bought a Bible. "I began to identify with Jesus. I felt he spent much of his time with people who were rejects, which I felt I was." Freeman was accepted into a circle of the church's men. He vividly remembers an occasion when, after he had picked up trash around the building, one of the men put an arm around him and said, "You did a really good job today."

"It was a job," Freeman said to me with a wistful smile, "which a seven-year-old can do." But he had never felt the approval of another man, never been part of male society. The warmth and acceptance of other men were changing his life. His desire for homosexuality and pornography began to wane.

Eventually he desired marriage. He felt no physical attraction to women, he said, but picked out "safe" girls to date. After several years he met his wife. "I was physically attracted to her. It was very new to me. I was surprised." They were married twelve years ago; they now have three children.

We drove to Freeman's home in suburban Philadelphia. His children were soon climbing over him. His wife, Penny, looked tired and glad to have some help. She is a pretty woman, with a graduate degree in counseling from Villanova.

While the children were in bed, we talked about the Freemans' married life. Both described the evening when, shortly before they were married, John told Penny of his homosexual past. "I hugged her, and she said, 'Your heart is beating at a thousand beats a second. What's wrong?' After I told her, she said, 'Do you think it will ever happen again?' I replied, 'As much as I know myself and my walk with the Lord, I don't think it will ever happen again.' "

It was his sincerity and gentleness that had attracted Penny to John. "I had a lot of confidence that he was a deep, sincere Christian." Wanting to believe that everything would work out, they married without further discussion of John's struggles. Their initial adjustment was easy.

We talked about a troubled period of their married life, after they had moved north so John could attend seminary. Within a year John's father and his best friend in Chattanooga died. John became deeply depressed, and homosexual feelings resurfaced. Though he did not succumb to the temptations, John sought counseling. He found it "very healing."

He had never intended to minister to homosexuals, but toward the end of his seminary education John sat in a class taught by urban missiologist Harvie Conn. Conn challenged his students to consider a mission to homosexuals. Freeman realized that without the warmth of his home church and without counseling, he might have been undone. Surely others were in the same situation. He wrote to everyone he knew, asking for their financial support. Quitting his job, he became Harvest's first staff member.

A crusading critic
From Philadelphia I took the train to Manhattan, to talk to the arch critic of the ex-gay movement, Ralph Blair. The founder of Evangelicals Concerned (EC), a group that promotes monogamous relationships between Christian homosexuals, Blair publishes a newsletter with his caustic reviews of evangelical books that discuss homosexuality, and a sarcastic diatribe against the ex-gay movement.

Apparently Blair is fiercer when seated at a word processor, for I found a small, mild man, neatly dressed in a coat and tie. Blair, a psychologist, told me that he works primarily with groups of homosexual men. He seemed grateful that I had come. He said no one from an evangelical publication had ever taken the time before. We talked more or less nonstop for the next seven hours.

Unlike many homosexuals I talked to, Blair said he had felt no great anxiety about his sexuality as an adolescent. He knew he was different, but, he said, "I just thought I was a slow developer." He became a Christian in junior high school and started college at Bob Jones University since it was the only Christian school he had ever heard of. He eventually graduated from Ball State University.

After some time at both Dallas and Westminster seminaries, he completed his theological studies at the University of Southern California, where he did a thesis on the ethics of euthanasia. Studying situational ethics led him to rethink his position on homosexuality. He eventually concluded that the Bible was not so absolute a voice on homosexuality as he had thought. He decided that the Bible's condemnations applied to the perversions of its day, not to a loving, committed relationship.

Then one evening, while staying up in order to attend a sunrise Easter service, he discovered for the first time in his life a gay bar. It was a room full of people whom he quickly identified as being very much like himself. "It was a good feeling," he told me. "I felt: Here is a place I belong." He said he experienced no great internal conflict with his faith. Any sense of guilt was swallowed up by the exhilaration of being among people who understood and accepted him for who he was.

The next fall he joined the staff of InterVarsity Christian Fellowship at the University of Pennsylvania. When IV officials realized what he was teaching, they asked him to resign. The next year he became a chaplain at Penn State. He stayed on to do a Ph.D. in psychology, studying the causes of homosexuality. Then he moved to New York, eventually to take up private therapy. In 1976 he founded EC and built a national network. He told me that he takes flak from both sides; to much of the New York gay community his opposition to promiscuity and his dogged determination to remain evangelical are anathema.

Blair's criticism of the ex-gay movement is absolute and unyielding. He regards their claims as sheer nonsense. He offered lists of former leaders who have dropped out. He painted a picture of a movement with a split personality—"living really promiscuous lives, which only reinforces why they should be preaching against homosexuality on Sunday." By contrast, he said, "My clients can go years without sex, because they're working toward an integrated, intimate relationship."

He urged me to listen carefully to how ex-gay leaders talked about marriage. "Ex-gays don't see marriage as necessarily including genital sex," he said. Most of their marriages were convenient living arrangements, he thought, but would never satisfy the need for erotic intimacy.

As we talked, I began to see that Blair accepts one of the tenets of modern life: that the need for erotic intimacy is close to the core of a human being. This is his understanding of God's word in Genesis, that it is "not good" for man to be alone. I offered my belief that the New Testament puts this in a different light, showing celibacy as a positive possibility. But it was clearly hard for him to perceive celibacy as anything but an option for a small minority of special people. He said he considers it callous and cruel for happily married people to deny others the possibility of intimate sex. "I think there is a gift of celibacy, but I don't think we should have the chutzpah to say everybody who is homosexual has that gift."

Blair, it seemed to me, was working from an argument that makes some sense in our modern therapeutic society, but none at all in biblical thinking: the claim that desires—particularly sexual desires—have a fundamental claim on us, and that those who cannot fulfill their desires must be unfulfilled.

But Blair obviously knew a lot about the ex-gay movement. He did not for a moment entertain the possibility of a changed sexual orientation. He portrayed an ex-gay movement that was all PR. After ten years in existence, said Blair, the movement ought to have legions of people whom it has helped. "Who are these 'lots of people' that have made it? Where are they?" Blair suggested that the leaders I was meeting were actually "falling" on a regular basis—if, in fact, they were truly homosexual in the first place. (Blair was using the common distinction between "real," exclusively homosexual persons, and those who are bisexual. It is a distinction that tends to exclude the possibility of change, since desires for the opposite sex would prove anyone to be bisexual, not a "real" homosexual.) Blair seemed generally to be a charitable man, but when he talked about the ex-gay movement, he grew sarcastic and angry.

I thought of John and Penny, whose home I had left that morning. They had seemed so vulnerable, almost incapable of putting on an act. The years of marriage, the stressed but happy family—was it an act? Anything is possible, but I found that hard to believe.

Blair invited me to walk up Park Avenue to his apartment. He seemed anxious to show me something. There, in an elegant, crowded living room, I saw a remarkable collection. Covering every wall, close together, were framed and matted signatures of evangelical heroes. Most were original signed personal letters. John and Charles Wesley, Moody, Sankey, Booth, Lewis, Chesterton, Sayers, Crosby, Sunday, Lightfoot, Newton, Wilberforce, Shaftesbury, and dozens of others were on display. For perhaps an hour, Blair took me carefully around the collection, explaining each one with obvious pride and love. "I don't get many chances to show these to someone who would appreciate them," he said.

Afterwards, on the train, I had melancholy thoughts of Ralph Blair. He had told me of being involved in two relationships, both of which ended when his lover left him. He is not strongly involved in any church, since most churches with a clear evangelical commitment find his stand unacceptable. And yet, he chooses to wake up every morning to what can only be called a museum of evangelicalism. He is determined to remain an evangelical; but more, he needs the warmth, the community of evangelicalism, and he has lost it.

Streams in the desert

Andy Comiskey is young, slender, smart, Irish, and very much a part of the meteoric Vineyard denomination. In recent years he has become the leading ex-gay theorist in Exodus. I went to see him particularly because I wanted to ask some of Ralph Blair's questions. We met at the Vineyard's sleek Santa Monica office—worlds apart from John Freeman's sparse environment. Later, while eating Greek food at a sidewalk table a few blocks from the beach, we talked.

Comiskey said that as an adolescent he had compensated for uneasiness about his masculinity by becoming a "funny, bright, androgenous character." In high school he had joined a group of friends who traveled regularly to the LA gay scene; during college he moved into a gay neighborhood. He had been raised Episcopalian, yet felt no great religious guilt about his homosexual activity. After years in the gay scene, however, he "began to feel a kind of bankruptcy." The gay community was full of warm, admirable people, but "I could see such a disparity between what they were seeking and what they were actually able to sustain. There was a goodness in them and a goodness in me that was being undermined."

He began a two-year pilgrimage out of the gay life into full Christian faith, a period in which he slipped back and forth between the gay and the church world. For three months he attended an ecumenical Bible study led by people who believed that God imposed no limits on homosexual behavior. Comiskey toyed with their ideas but ultimately decided they offered an impotent form of Christianity. Jesus, Comiskey thought, transformed lives; but these Christians presented their sexuality to Jesus as a *fait accompli*.

Like many ex-gay leaders I spoke to, Comiskey found that close, fraternal relationships were essential to his transformation. He lived in a UCLA Christian fraternity, where close quarters forced him to recognize his ambivalence toward other men. Then he attended the Santa Monica Vineyard church, experiencing the ministry of inner healing. He eventually became engaged to the woman he would marry and, at about the same time, started a Bible study that evolved into the Desert Streams ministry. It is one of the few ex-gay ministries that is an integral part of a church. Comiskey would like to see those ties proliferate.

I asked him Blair's question: Where are successes of the ex-gay ministries? Comiskey suggested they were blending into the church, as they should. He said he would be doubtful of any program that had ex-gays hanging around. In the average evangelical church, how likely was it that ex-gays would advertise their past?

When I asked about marriage, Comiskey said candidly that it was no panacea; ex-gay people often brought special problems to marriage, the product of years of distorted living. He said that sexual desire had not been a problem in his marriage, but it was for some.

I pressed the point: Did this mean they had really changed? Comiskey said, "Heterosexual desire is usually not an either/or thing." There are degrees of sexual attraction, which can change depending on other factors. For himself, he said, some homosexual desire continues; but when he is in affirming relationships with other men, there is no eroticism. "I don't believe that homosexuality is fundamentally erotic," he said. The erotic component grows out of insecurity in a person's own maleness or femaleness. Comiskey added that there can be an addictive element to sexual behavior: what you have grown used to, you tend to continue. These patterns have to be broken.

Comiskey was talking about real change, not merely adjustment to an unpleasant reality. He was not, however, talking about the conversion of homosexual men into *Playboy*-reading, macho American males. He said that many ex-gays gain an attraction to only one person of the opposite sex; they are not necessarily attracted to the opposite sex generally. (Other ex-gay leaders questioned whether generalized sexual attraction was all that positive a phenomenon.) Speaking personally, Comiskey said he felt some attraction to other women besides his wife; but he did not know how much this would expand as the years went by, and he did not seem terribly concerned that it should.

I came away with the sense that ex-gays and their critics sometimes talk past each other because they define homosexuality so differently. People in Ralph Blair's camp, on the one hand, see homosexuality almost as a third sex—an innate condition that is defined by erotic desire for one's own gender. Comiskey, on the other hand, insists that God created only two genders. Marriage is not essential, but healthy relating to the opposite sex is. There is no "third sex"—only distortions of the original two.

To Blair, desires prove your nature. He would believe ex-gay change was real only when ex-gay men ogled women on the beach. To Comiskey, a person's desires do not determine either one's identity or happiness: they are symptoms that shift gradually as a person becomes more secure in his or her real identity. Just as a man's erotic interest in *Playboy* does not prove him an inevitable adulterer, so a man's erotic interest in other men does not prove him inevitably homosexual. To Comiskey, desires come and go, proving vulnerability, not destiny.

What is real change?
One critic of the ex-gay movement, who asked to be anonymous because his income depended on evangelical respectability, described for me twenty years of trying to change his homosexual orientation, using every method from deliverance to electroshock therapy. Not only did his attempts fail, they left him utterly miserable. After attempting suicide five years ago, he abandoned the attempt, left his wife and children, and moved in with his male lover. He has joined the Metropolitan Community Church, a gay

church he said is thoroughly evangelical in every respect except its view of homosexuality.

When I first approached him, he did not want to talk at all. "There is no way that conservative Christian readers would listen to what I'm saying. They don't want to know what our lives are like. They want us to remain invisible." His whole life has been spent in hiding, and he blames the church.

I described to him what I had been hearing, that ex-gays developed a desire for one particular person, but not necessarily a generalized desire for the opposite sex. He scoffed at it. "That's what you say when you're near the end." True sexual desire is always general, he said.

Unlike Ralph Blair, he credited ex-gay leaders with sincerity, but felt they were sincerely deceived. "I have known twenty-five years of Andy Comiskeys," he told me. "I know the thrill of a burgeoning evangelical ministry. But he'll self-destruct. They all have, and they all will." This man considered Andy Comiskey, and others like him in the ex-gay movement, a menace. By offering a delusion, they lead others toward despair.

He and other critics attributed the growth of ex-gay ministries to widespread fear of AIDS. But ex-gay unreality would constantly catch up with the movement, they said.

Long-term success

Several times, to test the critics' assumptions of inevitable despair for ex-gay leaders, I brought up the name of Frank Worthen. Worthen left the gay life sixteen years ago after spending most of his adult life in it. The critics told me he must be repressing his deepest sexual needs—and hinted darkly that he might be leading a double life already.

Worthen has lead-colored hair, slicked straight·back, and glasses that are sometimes askew; he looks and talks like somebody you would meet in a Texas cafe instead of the successful San Francisco businessman that he is. With considerable dry humor he told me the story of how he had met his wife, Anita, at a time when he was contentedly celibate. He did not *seem* like a man who was repressing his deepest sexual needs.

Worthen admitted candidly that many of the leaders of the early ministries had dropped out. Recalling those days, he said they had all been naïve about the vulnerability of a person who, having just left a homosexual life, begins ministering to those who still tempt him, trying to meet enormous needs without adequate resources. Most of the early ex-gay ministries had no church ties or board oversight, and it was perhaps predictable that many flamed out. Exodus now has strict standards for ministries that want to affiliate, and Worthen believes they have left the difficulties of the early years behind. Bob Davies, who coordinates many of the Exodus activities, could not remember any leaders requiring discipline or intensive counseling in the last three years.

Worthen acknowledges that change is tough. But he is a tough sort of guy. He believes that if homosexuals are willing to change, and have adequate support, their lives can be transformed.

Hope and caution

I went doubtful; I came away with a cautious optimism. I think a significant movement is happening. Ex-gay ministries may end up teaching us all lessons of Christian discipleship in the realm of sexual desire.

The ex-gay leaders I talked to seemed as open, sincere, and vulnerable as any individuals I have interviewed. I don't doubt that many currents swirl yet inside them, some of which they do not understand and cannot control. (I would say the same of myself.) And sexual currents are strong. Yet, overall, the ex-gay leaders I talked to left an impression of health.

They were certainly not describing a quick, 180-degree reversal of their sexual desires; rather, they described a gradual reversal in their spiritual understanding of themselves as men and women in relationship to God. They said this new understanding was helping them to relearn distorted patterns of thinking and relating. They presented themselves as people in process, though they were very clear that the process was well under way.

Within this kind of understanding, it is not surprising that some ex-gays struggle and fall and struggle again, just as other Christians do when they deal with heterosexual promiscuity, or alcoholism, or greed, or anger. The degrees of healing vary. But the possibility of living an adjusted, hopeful, and fruitful life in a sin-distorted world—and the possibility of growing more joyful and consistent in that life—remains.

Two words of caution still need to be made, however: First, the ex-gay movement is young, small, and operates in unknown territory. Theological correctness does not guarantee them success. All ministry is risk, and this kind is more risky than most.

Second, the ex-gay movement comprises many tiny ministries operating in a kind of spread-out ghetto. The wider church has them in a quarantine, waiting to see whether they will slip up. Lacking much tangible or emotional support from the larger body of Christ, they are peculiarly vulnerable. The church's quarantine could be a self-fulfilling prophecy.

People with homosexual desire need the church's concern. Many desperately want help from a church, but they are afraid to identify themselves for fear of being ostracized. Most congregations know nothing about the needs of homosexuals, and many do not want to know.

Ex-gay ministries offer a way to respond. If the wider church were to embrace such ministries, it would see at close range the realism of what they do. If the church keeps them at arm's length, it will never know. They will be weaker. The rest of us will be, too.

Chapter 5

MINISTRY OUTSIDE THE CHURCH

Ronald Enroth

During the past two decades, there have emerged outside mainstream Christian denominations a number of organizations and churches dedicated to serving the spiritual needs of the homophile community. These groups vary greatly in their objectives, theology, and attitudes toward the larger Christian community. Some define themselves as activist/advocacy groups functioning in an unofficial capacity as gay adjuncts to conventional denominations. Others have few ties with organized religion and maintain low visibility even within the gay subculture. At least one—the Metropolitan Community Church—has achieved quasi-denominational status. A few of them identify with evangelicalism and view their ministry as an outreach to both non-Christians and Christians who are struggling with the issue of homosexuality.

Regardless of their positions on such questions as the origin and nature of same-sex relations and whether or not homosexuals can be "cured," nearly all those involved in ministry to gays (or ex-gays) admit that their task has been made more difficult by the attitudes and atmosphere generated by "straight" Christians and conventional churches. The primary reason for the emergence of ministries outside the parameters of traditional Christianity—both liberal and conservative—has been the pattern of rejection, hostility, and lack of compassionate understanding that so often characterizes the church's orientation toward homosexuals. Gay people believe that their confusion, hurts, and loneliness are often painfully compounded by insensitive Christians who view homosexual disorder very differently from heterosexual vulnerability.

When they feel rejected by both secular society and traditional religion, what are some of the groups that homosexuals turn to?

Ministries to gays and ex-gays
Homosexuals Anonymous. This nationwide self-help group was founded in 1980 by Colin, a former minister, and Doug, a former school principal (HA members use only their first names when they refer publicly to their association with HA). HA is modeled after Alcoholics Anonymous and uses a fourteen-step program to assist people in overcoming their homosexual urges. Five of the steps are drawn from AA, while the other nine stem from Colin's and Doug's personal insights.

HA is a lay organization with a small network of chapters throughout the country and a few overseas. Groups are organized individually but receive help through training seminars that the service center (Homosexuals Anonymous Fellowship Services) provides across the country. The fellowship governs itself through a board of directors and an annual HA conference. HA is also unique among the "anonymous" groups in that it is the only overtly Christ-centered anonymous group, recognizing that the redemptive work of Christ provides a new identity and power for freedom for the homosexual struggler. Although HA is a "step" program, it is rooted in a very careful psychological application of the gospel.

HA maintains that God created all men and women heterosexual. Homosexuality is understood to be a confused gender identity brought on by an emotionally wounded childhood, an addiction to sexual escapes from the emotional pain, and a spiritual delusion that has led the struggler to fear God and misidentify his or her problem. HA support groups help men and women examine their confusion, discover their true identity, and break from compulsive habits that hinder their healing and growth as children of God.

Love in Action. This evangelical ministry to people affected by homosexuality has been operating out of San Rafael, California, for many years. Director Frank Worthen oversees an organization that includes counseling, a live-in program for men and women, and a teaching/educational outreach to the Christian community. Love in Action is committed to the proposition that people can be delivered from homosexuality and that the church is to be God's healing agent.

Lutherans Concerned/North America. Founded in 1974, this Chicago-based group is directed at Lutherans and other Christians who are either gays/lesbians or supportive heterosexuals. Its stated objective is to create a climate of justice, reconciliation, and understanding among all men and women, whatever their affectional preference. It encourages the church to deal honestly, objectively, and openly with the concerns and problems of gay people within the church and those who have left the church.

Courage. Father John Harvey founded *Courage* in the middle 1960s. This Roman Catholic group (New York City) functions as a spiritual support group for Catholic homosexuals. Members are urged to resist homosexual behavior and either lead celibate lives or move to heterosexual development. They model their program after the twelve steps of AA.

Affirmation: United Methodists for Lesbian/Gay Concerns. Founded in 1976, this organization provides educational and informational services and affirms all individuals in the United Methodist Church regardless of race, class, age, sex, or sexual orientation. It is involved in ecumenical and interfaith activity and operates a justice ministry on behalf of victims of discrimination.

LIFE. A nondenominational Christian ministry, LIFE (Living in Freedom Eternally) believes homosexuality is a psychological disorder that can be healed through a personal relationship with Jesus Christ. LIFE offers counseling services, support groups, and educational seminars.

New Ways Ministry. This Roman Catholic gay/lesbian ministry provides information concerning homosexuality in the Catholic church and encourages theological dialogue. It also sponsors workshops, seminars, and retreats.

Integrity. Consisting of gay and lesbian Episcopalians and their supporters, Integrity provides a variety of services to clergy and lay persons, including conferences, counseling, and AIDS ministries. One of the group's objectives is to promote the full participation of gay people in church and society.

Outpost. Founder and director Ed Hurst operates a Christian counseling service in the Minneapolis–St. Paul area. A born-again Christian, Hurst believes homosexuals can overcome their lifestyle, if not their orientation.

Evangelicals Concerned. Founder and president Ralph Blair attended several well-known evangelical seminaries and was once on the staff of InterVarsity Christian Fellowship. He is critical of the traditional evangelical stance toward homosexuality, claiming that evangelicals oppress and mistreat homosexuals, and offer only "nonhelp." His group calls on evangelicals to act responsibly and realistically with homosexuals.

Dignity. The oldest and largest organization of its kind, Dignity is composed of gay and lesbian Roman Catholics, with a nationwide membership of about 5,000. Until Vatican officials cracked down in the late 1980s, Dignity had been allowed to hold special masses in many dioceses. Dignity has three main objectives: to affirm that it is possible for Catholics to be both gay and Christian; to work within the church to redefine its theology of sex; and to correct injustices within the church and society. Dignity has responded to Rome's pressure by declaring that "gay and lesbian people can express their sexuality physically, in a creative manner that is loving, life-giving and life-affirming."[1]

Whatever the goals and specific programs of these various organizations and ministries, there is one crucial question that each must address—one that usually places them in opposing camps. It is the issue of how they view homosexuality, specifically homosexual practice, in the light of biblical faith, and how that understanding relates to the possibility of making a transition out of homosexuality into exclusive heterosexuality. Is homosexuality a gift of God to be affirmed, or is it a manifestation of human fallenness and confused sexual identity in need of redemption and healing?

These issues are complex and discussed more fully elsewhere in this book, but they are focal concerns of all those who minister to gay men and lesbian women, both within the church and outside its immediate circle. Having briefly surveyed some of these outreaches, we can now examine more closely two organizations with very different aims and radically different perspectives: the Metropolitan Community Church and Desert Stream Ministries. Both have been acclaimed as successful; both consider themselves to be Christian organizations involved in ministry to homosexuals; and each views the other as controversial.

The Metropolitan Community Church

The Universal Fellowship of Metropolitan Community Churches (UFMCC) is a quasi-denomination of more than 30,000 worshipers in over 250 congregations in North America and abroad. The Metropolitan Community Church represents the largest "gay church" in the world, with its own theological seminary in Los Angeles to train men and women for a variety of ministries, including special outreach programs to prisoners, AIDS victims, substance abusers, and Spanish-speaking gays.

With the advent of the AIDS epidemic, some MCC pastors are devoting half their time to AIDS-related activities. "We have come to understand ourselves as a church with AIDS. This doesn't mean that our church will soon be dead and gone. . . . Many people are seeking intimacy and spirituality, which has had the effect of a revival.

Thus, despite the deaths of many members, our membership has actually grown. . . ."[2]

In 1968, Troy D. Perry, a former Pentecostal preacher, founded the MCC in Los Angeles. Twelve people attended the first service, which was held in the living room of Perry's house. In his book *The Lord Is My Shepherd and He Knows I'm Gay*, Perry describes what he told those first parishioners:

> I said the church was organized to serve the religious and spiritual and social needs of the homosexual community of greater Los Angeles, but I expected it to grow to reach homosexuals wherever they might be. I made it clear that we were not a gay church; we were a Christian church, and I said that in my first sermon.[3]

Despite Perry's initial intentions, the Metropolitan Community Church has not been able to shed its image as the "gay church." The MCC proclaims that it is "just like any other Christian church," and it is advertised as being a church for "all people." However, MCC and many other gay religious groups are merely an ecclesiastical extension of the secular gay subculture. Its linkage with the gay liberation movement and other socio-political advocacy groups is obvious. MCC sees itself in the forefront of those fighting oppression and homophobia with the added advantage that "God is on our side." It is a variation on the familiar theme, "We may stand condemned in the courts of men but not before the throne of God." By appealing to God for his stamp of approval, gay Christians are adopting a mode of response that sociologists call "stigma redemption."

That is *not* to say that MCC leadership and laypersons are insincere in their desire to minister to the spiritual needs of gay people. There can be no question that MCC is accomplishing much good, particularly in its ministry to people with AIDS (commonly referred to as PWAs). As Howard Wells, founding pastor of MCC–San Francisco and himself a PWA, noted, "The specter of AIDS catapults us into accelerated spiritual growth—or toward early death—and it all depends on the model of eschatological living we choose to follow."[5]

Evangelical critics see MCC engaging in a form of theological-deviance neutralization not unlike the attempts of secular gays to promote homosexuality as an "alternative lifestyle." That is to say, MCC puts forth an image of nondeviance by redefining what has been traditionally viewed as deviant behavior rather than advocating that individuals can change. At the core of this redefinition process is MCC's theology of human sexuality. Gay Christians contend that sexuality is neither right nor wrong, it is simply a gift from God.

> To be heterosexual or homosexual is not a question of sin or morality, but rather the product of God's infinite mind. For reasons unknown he has assigned all of mankind to one of the two sexual roles. Our only responsibility is to accept his decision. . . . The gay person therefore must be enlightened to the point of accepting his sexual orientation. He must "come out," no longer hiding his homosexuality with shame but rather pronouncing it boldly and with pride.[6]

Because MCC spokespersons view homosexuality as genetically and divinely caused, they argue that it would be unnatural and against God's will to attempt to change a person's sexual orientation. Furthermore, to deny a gay person any form of sexual expression is unthinkable. Troy Perry believes a theology of sexuality does not include "a list of do's and don'ts for sexual activity or anything else. That would be silly. We are hoping it can be a guide to how we can use our sexuality to advance our spiritual awareness, how we can use our sexuality to please God."[7]

MCC and similar progay ministries have developed a theological stance that becomes a mechanism for reconciling and justifying obviously contradictory views. The result, according to Carl F. H. Henry, is that "biblical condemnations of homosexuality become a jungle of nonsense." Henry notes that the homosexual "fails to understand that the Spirit of God transforms all men into the moral image of Jesus Christ and not the church into the image of the gay world. . . . What the gay world needs is redemption, not reinforcement."[8]

In its official publications, in its political-action efforts, and in social activities, the MCC often reflects and reinforces aspects of the secular gay subculture. Though the gay church attempts to promote an image of being a "typical Christian church," the trappings of the gay world often overshadow the ostensibly religious nature of the organization. "The only real difference between the gay world of the homosexual church and the secular gay world is that the former includes a religious or spiritual dimension that often appears to be tacked on in an attempt at securing moral legitimacy for homosexual behavior."[9]

The MCC attempts to confer legitimation on same-sex relationships by formalizing those relationships in solemn rites of holy union. The denomination's bylaws describe this ritual as "the spiritual joining of two persons in a manner fitting and proper by a duly authorized minister of the church."[10] Although the rite has no legal sanction, it is another example of how the MCC tries to achieve "legitimation by association." Interestingly, the phrase " 'til death do us part," is seldom found in the holy union vows. MCC ministers prefer something more realistic, like, "as long as love lasts."[11] MCC pastors also perform a "blessing of intention"—a rite similar to the Roman Catholic posting of marriage banns—for couples of the same sex.

Desert Stream Ministries

As a young Christian confronting the complexity of his homosexuality, Andrew Comiskey was introduced to a group of earnest gays at the Metropolitan Community Church. Their testimonies moved him, and he was attracted to the possibility of enjoying the best of both worlds—the blessings of faith and the opportunity for homosexual intimacy. His commentary on MCC's brand of spirituality, however, is revealing:

> But something struck me in their stories that seemed inherently alien to the gospel. Little, if any, glory was given to the transforming power of Jesus. . . . These pro-gay Christians were expressing more of the glory of their gayness than the honor of Jesus. Their homosexuality was no longer submitted to His scrutiny but held fast as a kind of personal right. In short, I intuited a profound lack of inspiration in their faith. However wounded by the church and sincere in trying to heal the pain, these pilgrims were not anointed.[12]

Andrew Comiskey's journey eventually included study at Fuller Theological Seminary as well as the opportunity to begin Desert Stream Ministries, a uniquely effective outreach of counseling and healing to homosexuals and others suffering from broken sexuality. Desert Stream, with its in-depth program known as Living Waters, is a model of empathetic, Christ-centered, compassionate ministry that is both outside the church and yet vitally linked to a local fellowship of believers. The Vineyard Christian Fellowship of Santa Monica, California, initially nourished Desert Stream before it became an independent ministry. Desert Stream is also linked with Exodus, an international coalition of ministries for homosexuals discussed in chapters three and four of this book. The philosophy and methodology of Desert Stream, as well as Andrew Comiskey's own story of struggle and victory, is told in his remarkable book, *Pursuing Sexual Wholeness: How Jesus Heals the Homosexual.*

The word *struggler* is perhaps the most frequently used term in Comiskey's book. It underscores his assertion that the road to restoration and wholeness is a gradual process, one characterized by a love that progressively frees strugglers to relate intimately but nonerotically to people of their own gender. Correspondingly, the Desert Stream program helps them develop the capacity to relate to people of the opposite sex in a healthy way, not in fear or with distaste.

At the core of Desert Stream's approach is the understanding that freedom from homosexuality involves a personal, powerful relationship with Christ coupled with recognition of the need for fellowship within his church.

> . . . [W]e ask each struggler, Where is God in your homosexual struggle? Is He alive and well and standing with you? . . . [W]hen strugglers discover the Father's supportive love, they find new hope. No longer are they alone, knowing where they should be but living a lie. . . . The Creator reveals Himself as One who does more than just determine sexual order; He also comes alongside and grants the one caught in the assurance of greater realities ahead.[13]

Desert Stream Ministries offers a twenty-lesson program of intensive healing and discipleship that enables strugglers to identify their needs, submit to Jesus for healing, and be part of an accountability structure as they grow toward wholeness and the reframing of their sexual identity. A small-group format combined with the importance of corporate worship is central to the program. The guidebook used by program participants outlines the goals of Living Waters as follows:

1. To help you embrace Jesus as the Lord and healer of your sexuality, your advocate as opposed to your adversary, in your struggle to be free.
2. To help you understand the deep and painful roots of your homosexual struggle.
3. To help you turn from sinful and destructive expressions of your homosexual struggle.
4. To help you to identify and receive the deep healing Jesus offers you at the core of your sexual identity.
5. To help you work out this healing by developing whole relationships with both men and women within the body of Christ.[14]

Andrew Comiskey and his staff balance biblical and spiritual considerations with insights gained from the medical and behavioral sciences. They recognize that social, psychological, and spiritual factors affect our sexuality. If sexual confusion is learned, they maintain, it can also be unlearned. Sexual disorder is understood in the context of a fallen, broken world, but God's unlimited power is available to bring about the realignment of desire that is fundamental to the healing process. "Homosexual strugglers who seek freedom thus exemplify honesty about personal weakness and an openness to God's renewal. They become true supernaturalists. The order and wholeness of their lives depend on One greater who lives in them."[15]

Gay people, professionals, and even evangelical Christians continue to debate the efficacy of programs designed to help homosexuals change their orientation. Andrew Comiskey and the folks at Desert Stream Ministries serve as an impressive model to demonstrate that God can reorient the struggler who truly submits and that Jesus will be glorified in the honest testimony of those who have become whole. They would agree with Jack and Judith Balswick, who wrote:

Homosexuals and heterosexuals alike must strive to find a wholeness in their lives in a less than ideal world. We all struggle in our own ways for sexual authenticity. We believe that God can lead each one of us closer to sexual wholeness. This will of course be a more painful and difficult process for some than for others, but Christ is willing to grant to all the privilege of walking through that process with him.[16]

Notes

1. *Time* magazine, December 5, 1988, p. 60.
2. Kittredge Cherry and James Mitulski, "We Are the Church Alive, the Church with AIDS," *The Christian Century*, January 27, 1988, p. 86.
3. Troy D. Perry, *The Lord Is My Shepherd and He Knows I'm Gay* (Los Angeles: Nash Publishing, 1972), p. 122.
4. See Ronald M. Enroth, "The Homosexual Church: An Ecclesiastical Extension of a Subculture," *Social Compass*, XXI, No. 3, 1974, 355–60.
5. Cherry and Mitulski, p. 86.
6. Ronald M. Enroth and Gerald E. Jamison, *The Gay Church* (Grand Rapids: Eerdmans, 1974), p. 41.
7. Jim Seale, "The Gay Reformation," *New Age Journal*. March 1985, p. 65.
8. Carl F. H. Henry, "In and Out of the Gay World," in *Is Gay Good?* ed. W. Dwight Oberholtzer (Philadelphia: Westminster Press, 1971), p. 109.
9. Enroth and Jamison, p. 113.
10. Quoted in "Community News," a quarterly newsletter from Metropolitan Community Church of San Francisco: Winter, 1980–81.
11. Ibid.
12. Andrew Comiskey, *Pursuing Sexual Wholeness* (Lake Mary, Fla.: Creation House, 1989), p. 26.
13. Ibid., pp. 49 and 51–52.
14. Andrew Comiskey, *Guidebook to Pursuing Sexual Wholeness* (Santa Monica, Calif.: Desert Stream Ministries, 1988), p. 11.

15. Comiskey, *Pursuing Sexual Wholeness*, p. 198.

16. Jack Balswick and Judith Balswick, *The Family* (Grand Rapids: Baker Book House, 1989), p. 189.

Chapter 6

HOOKED ON SEX

David Neff

What are the implications of the sexual addiction movement for ministry to homosexuals?

I t was the AIDS scare that finally got to Nigel (not his real name). When the grim reaper's scythe cut down Nigel's friends, turning their lovely, muscular bodies to cadaverous frames, his homosexual romanticism was shattered. It was then he sought the help that finally turned his life around and broke his cyclical pattern of indulgence in the excesses of the gay lifestyle that had alternated with periods of remorseful self-control.

Nigel had tried to quit many times: in Bible college, in the ministry, in a public-service career; through counseling, through prayer, through self-control. But independent of his will, the covert life of his Mr. Hyde went on.

At work, his focus was blurred by his daydreams of naked bodies in a steam room, and his creativity was drained by demanding activities of the night before. Yet his poor performance did not drive him to change. The threat of being exposed seemed only to add a degree of exhilaration to his escapades. And even his burning shame seemed only to drive him to seek greater solace in the anonymous intimacy of the gay scene.

Somehow, AIDS made the difference. The sight of withering bodies shocked him to his senses. And with the help of a therapist, a spiritual guide, and an accepting church, Nigel made a clean break with his delusional thinking and his destructive behavior.

Addictions in different guises
Looking back on his experience, Nigel can say he was hooked on sex. Some clinicians would call his affliction "sexual addiction." The most prominent clinician to popularize the idea of sexual addiction is Patrick Carnes, who designed the in-patient program for sexual dependency at the Golden Valley Health Center in Minneapolis. His books, *Out of the Shadows: Understanding Sexual Addiction* and *Contrary to Love: Helping the Sexual Addict*, are invaluable for understanding the power that sexual indulgence seems to have over many of those we know and love.[1] Dr. Carnes's writings are the basis for much of what follows.

The language of addiction, traditionally reserved for chemical dependency, is today being applied to nearly every imaginable behavioral problem. Some observers find it amusing to think of such behaviors as shopping and jogging being treated like addictions; on the other hand, many behavioral professionals find the trend profoundly irritating, because the addictions movement is led largely by lay people who could easily miss signals of a serious disturbance that might require hospitalization or drug therapy.

Nevertheless, in many cases the realization of being hooked on sex—in the same way some people become hopelessly dependent on alcohol or some other drug—can be the catalyst that brings together the people, the resources, the accountability, the insight, and the will to change.

To understand why people are talking about "sexual addiction," it is necessary to identify just what we mean by an addiction. Addictions come in different guises. Following the work of H. Milkman and M. Sunderwirth, we can divide them into three categories: (1) "arousal addictions" (amphetamines, gambling, taking risks, sex); (2) "satiation addictions" (alcohol, depressive drugs, compulsive overeating); and (3) "fantasy addictions" (artistic obsessions, mystical states, marijuana, and psychedelics).[2] Thus addiction is a many-splintered thing. And many addicts have multiple addictions—sex and alcohol being one of the most common combinations. Despite all this variety, there are behavioral patterns that tie this collection of addictions together. Here, in broad outline, is a list of the self-defeating behavior patterns and delusional ways of thinking that can characterize any addict, including a sex addict:

Addicts have lost the ability to say no—in spite of serious consequences. Sex addicts cannot say no to sex. It may seem to them that someone else, an evil Mr. Hyde, is making choices for them. Not only have they lost the ability to say no to particular sexual activities, they have lost the ability to say no to sexual ideas and daydreams. Nigel, for example, spent most of his time physically at work, but he was mentally unable to concentrate on the demands of his job. He was obsessed with the thought of whom he might meet and what they might do when he got off work. The limits most people face—money, time, work, and family demands—mean little to addicts. Even when these limits are tightly drawn about them, if they can at all say yes, they will not say no.

Addicts very likely have a secret life and can go to extreme efforts to maintain appearances. Sex addicts often live double lives: they carefully build walls between the world of work and family on the one hand, and the world of sexual exploitation on the other. During one period of his life, Nigel drove sixty-five miles almost every night after work for an anonymous plunge into the gay-bar scene. Yet, during the rest of the time, Nigel appeared not only respectable but highly religious. Later Nigel moved into one of our largest metropolitan areas. There he was able to disappear into the homosexual culture, but always with the fear he might unexpectedly meet someone who would recognize him from his work, church, or family connections. What Nigel dreaded most was being discovered.

The behavior of addicts goes in cycles. Sex addicts often go through periods of rigid control alternating with times of extended indulgence. Shame or remorse or simple consequences can bring a period of indulgence to a close. After weeks or months of indulgence, Nigel would be able to achieve the appearance of freedom. The behavior of sex addicts can de-escalate, and addicts seem to have gained control. It is likely, however, that they very likely are now obsessed with keeping sex under control—and in that state they are like the taut spring on a mousetrap, just waiting for some catalytic event to trigger their addiction.

Addicts are often subject to feelings of shame and remorse, and occasionally they may become severely depressed or suicidal. Because their behavior often violates social norms, as well as their own sense of right and wrong, sex addicts often feel deeply ashamed of their behavior. But sex addicts do not have to have a religious upbringing, as Nigel did, to feel guilt and remorse. It is tempting to blame religion—particularly for people who were raised in a fundamentalist or traditional Catholic context—for the crippling shame they might experience. But research shows that sex addicts often come from dysfunctional families where they learned early to have very low opinions of themselves. Such a family background can produce paralyzing guilt better than anything religion has ever devised.

Addicts have lost the ability to think straight. Sex addicts can ignore the truth of their bank book and spend nonexistent money on pornography and prostitution. Sex addicts can engage in hours of sexual activity and other debauchery at night and irrationally believe they will be fresh and alert enough to do their work in the morning. Some sex addicts can ignore what they see in the mirror and believe themselves to be unusually virile or physically seductive. Other sex addicts can ignore all their attractive and good qualities and believe themselves to be basically worthless human beings. Whatever thought pattern serves the addiction is likely to dominate over clear thinking and common sense.

Addicts put their addiction first, often manipulating and betraying friendships and work responsibilities to feed their lust. Sex addicts lie. Sex addicts cheat. Sex addicts steal. Sex addicts break promises. "I've learned my lesson." "I won't do it again." "I'll pay you back on payday." "I love you." Sex addicts say all those things—and they may think they mean them. Persons raised in dysfunctional families, as a disproportionate number of sex addicts are, often have problems knowing whom to trust and how to be close. Thus they learn to depend on themselves for themselves. The power of their addictive mindset means that sex comes first, that their perceived responsibility to themselves comes first, and that others can adjust or wait or "go to hell." In this way, addictive persons behave like psychopaths.

The core beliefs of addiction
All of these behavioral patterns that describe addiction in general (and sex addiction in particular) are based on four core beliefs: (1) I am basically a bad, unworthy person. (2) No one would love me as I am. (3) My needs are never going to be met if I have to depend on others. (4) Sex is my most important need.

These core beliefs often arise from childhood experiences. Perhaps a person's family of origin was cold and distant. Perhaps that family was "rigidly enmeshed"—that is, the family members were so closely involved and their identities so determined by their membership in the family that the children had no room to experiment, explore, and discover who they were. Perhaps the child was abandoned—through actual abandonment, or perhaps through death or divorce. Any of these situations, and many others, could produce or reinforce the first three core beliefs: unworthiness, unlovability, and inability to form trusting relationships. The first three core beliefs can form the foundation of an addictive pattern. They await the final ingredient that can form a person into an addict of a particular type.

Nancy felt abandoned. The birth mother she never knew had given her up for adoption. The family that adopted her was affluent, prominent in the community, and conventionally religious. Unfortunately, discipline was erratic and abusive. When, like all teens, she violated the limits her parents had set, they would explode, putting on an extreme emotional display. They would threaten dire punishments, which they rarely delivered. When Nancy regularly overdrew her checking account, they would rage. But after the emotional display, they would quietly cover the bounced checks rather than make her work to pay for her mistakes. Occasionally, her father would lose his temper and beat her. But after the abuse, her mother would buy her something special, something expensive. Perhaps because of the feelings of abandonment and the yo-yo relationships with her adopted parents, Nancy felt no emotional warmth toward them or from them or her adopted brothers. She felt bad, unworthy, and unlovable. Above all, she felt she could not trust anyone.

Nancy had the first three of the addict's core beliefs firmly in place. When her adopted brothers forced her to have sex with them, the die was cast. Sex became for her the door to intimacy, or the closest thing she could imagine to intimacy. It was, however, loaded with a mixture of associations. It implied closeness and pleasure; but it also implied alienation and pain. In being sexual, she felt warmth and acceptance mixed with shame and fear. Nevertheless, she began to exhibit cyclical indulgence in illicit sexuality. Periodically deciding to reform, she would seek out her pastor or a particular friend who was known for being both a "straight arrow" and a "Good Samaritan." At other times, she tried to interrupt the cycle of compulsive sexuality by attempting suicide or threatening murder. Had Nancy been seduced by a female authority figure who also showed her tenderness and affection, her addiction might have taken the form of lesbianism.

In any case, a dysfunctional family background sets the stage for addiction. The catalytic events and relationships help to determine the shape of that relationship. While little information other than anecdotal material exists on sex addicts' families of origin, some study has been made of the nature of sex offenders' families during their teen years. Many sex offenders show symptoms of addictive illness. When asked to rate their perceptions of their families on a dependency (trust) scale ranging from the chaotic (no accountability for sexual behavior, discrepancies between values and behavior, etc.) to the rigid (unreachable expectations, extreme efforts to control child's sexual behavior), the vast majority of the sex offenders studied (77 percent) rated their families as clearly rigid. When asked to rate their families on an intimacy scale from extreme disengagement (emotional abandonment, evasion of sexual issues) to enmeshment (anxiety about sexual behavior reflecting on family, secrecy preserved, covert sexual abuse), 57 percent rated the families of their teen years as disengaged. Normal adolescents, when given a similar evaluation, tended to rate their families in the middle of the scale (47 percent called their families balanced, and another 34 percent rated their families in the midrange). By way of contrast, among the sex offenders only 11 percent rated their families balanced, while 49 percent placed their families in the extreme ranges.[3] It becomes clear that a family's balance (or lack of balance) on intimacy and dependency issues can have an important effect on a young person's sexual development.

Getting beyond *don't*

Ask almost any gay who grew up in a Christian context, and he will tell you how his church responded to homosexuality: It said "don't." He will also tell you how unhelpful that was. The negative focus may merely perpetuate the obsession with sexual acting out. That obsession will now take the form of an agonizing effort at control, but the inner slavery to the lust remains.

Although not every homosexual is a sex addict, a large number of those who present themselves to ex-gay ministries, pastors, counselors, or others for help are likely to suffer from some form of compulsive illness. Certainly, some who come for help are those who simply feel bad about their sexual orientation and want to change. But many are at the point of unmanageability in the addictive cycle—the point where exposure, financial ruin, job loss, or marriage breakdown become so threatening that, despite delusional thinking patterns, the addict makes a desperate effort to seek help.

Because the church is often seen as being concerned primarily with morals, and because great shame and guilt feelings are attached to homosexual activity, persons who seek help will very likely approach the subject in the moral terms they believe ministers will understand. A minister should articulate the message of God's love and grace. But it would be a mistake for a minister to focus the first interviews on the morality of homosexuality. If the person already feels shame and guilt, merely hearing the representative of the church articulate once again its condemnation will not bring any change in the addict's situation. (Likewise, the opposite extreme of the liberal spirit, assuring the deeply pained person that modern science has shown that his orientation is just one among many, does not move him along the path toward healing.)

When sexual addicts reach a crisis of unmanageability, they often go into a period of de-escalation in which rigid control is exerted on the sexual acting out. The obsession with sex remains; it has only inverted. There is no freedom here. Carnes is worth quoting at some length:

> The moralistic church, in its battle to control the lust-driven sinner, shares a common element with the addict: obsession. The battlefield becomes a narrow continuum in which the only options are to be good or to be bad, to be saved or to be damned. Excluded are spirituality, responsibility, and the joy of sexual expression.
>
> ... Those addicts who subscribe to the narrow model of good versus evil—essentially a model built on shame and control—may return to the church. They may become not only pillars of the church community but avenging angels out to destroy all lust. ...
>
> For other addicts whose religious experiences have at best been peripheral, it may be a time for conversion experiences. Their conversion significantly occurs immediately after a major unmanageability event such as an arrest. Unfortunately, they may adopt wholesale the belief system of their new community in place of a thoughtful, long-term spiritual pilgrimage that integrates a new understanding with integrity. ... [Caught in a cycle of conversion experiences,] he will successfully resist any rehabilitation efforts aimed at making his recovery the fundamental issue. Instead of looking for peace and forgiveness, the crusader and the instant convert find a place to hide. When pastoral counselors become aware of this ploy, they can guide the addict toward a program of true recovery.[4]

One leader in ex-gay ministry says it's not very difficult at all to distinguish Carnes's "instant convert." "In nearly all cases," he says, "conversion simply is a control stage. And if further Christian maturity doesn't take place, it is simply going to be control until maybe eight or nine months down the road. The person gets disappointed because he thinks conversion is going to completely eliminate the problem."

"We recognize very easily the homosexual equivalent of a dry drunk," says this minister. "The person shows clear body language of panic and anxiety, and he can't talk healthily and positively about sex. He can't even bring up the themes very well. He can't use the words—he is simply in a state of repression."

Instead of focusing on homosexual feelings or acting out, the minister or counselor is wise to explore factors in the addict's life that could underlie the addict's four core beliefs. Does the person feel bad, dirty, worthless? (It usually doesn't take much questioning to determine the person's feelings at this point. This material is often expressed both verbally and in body language at the beginning of the interview.) Does the person feel unloved and unlovable? Does the person feel he or she cannot trust or depend on anyone? ("Has anyone important in your life ever really let you down?") What does the person think is his or her most important need? ("When you feel discouraged, or when you feel you have something disappointing happen, what do you do to help yourself feel better?")

These lines of questioning will offer signals as to whether the problem may be sexual addiction. A thorough history of sexual activity is necessary before a final judgment is made, but this may be difficult to achieve. Addicts are liars, and above all they lie to themselves. They do not want to admit to addictive patterns, and without an ongoing trusting relationship, the minister or counselor will have a difficult time establishing an accurate account of the person's activity. Nevertheless, it is worth asking the person to keep a journal and, at least for his or her own eyes, write out a sexual history. Many find this homework to be a fascinating assignment.

Addicts by definition are people who do not trust. Because Nancy had difficulty believing she could depend on her minister and her "straight arrow" friend, she tested them regularly. In conversations she would forthrightly challenge their friendship, forcing them to say they would never let her down. She would periodically call them (often late at night) after having gotten herself into difficult circumstances. She threatened one of them with a gun. The other she tried to seduce. She attempted suicide by combining alcohol and pills, and as she was passing out, she gave a bystander her pastor's telephone number.

Fortunately for Nancy, her pastor and her friend stood by her but did not coddle her. They called the police and reported the pistol incident. They had her admitted to a psychiatric ward following the suicide attempt. Sexual advances were met with flat refusals. Her trust-testing behavior was identified for what it was.

Anyone ministering to persons who may be sexual addicts has to be prepared for this testing of relationships. It takes a long time to break down the dependency and emotional intimacy barriers built up through childhood. If the person remains (as Nancy did) in her family system where the core beliefs are rooted, it may be well nigh impossible for a minister to facilitate a breakthrough. Reaching for such change requires working with the entire family, a highly unlikely opportunity in many religious communities where the family's respectability is highly valued.

Fortunately, a better way is now widely available. Over the past ten years, "Twelve-Step Groups" have proliferated. These are groups that have applied the principles of Alcoholics Anonymous to the sundry addictions experienced in modern life. For sex addicts and their families, specific groups go by names such as Sexaholics Anonymous, Sex and Love Addicts Anonymous, Sexual Addicts Anonymous, and Sexual Abuse Anonymous. For those who wish to conquer their addiction and turn away from a homosexual orientation, there is Homosexuals Anonymous. These groups have in their own ways adapted AA's Twelve Steps. Homosexuals Anonymous has made some substitutions and expansions with biblical material to create its Fourteen Steps.

These groups are not unified. The very nature of "anonymous" groups prevents any kind of national structure, standardization, or "quality control." Yet they promise and deliver significant change for many with compulsive illness.

The "magic" of the Twelve Steps
Many conservative Christians are vexed by the trend toward calling alcoholism and compulsive sexuality "addictions" and "illnesses." They are afraid such labels remove the moral stigma from the behavior and the moral responsibility from the person who indulges in these behaviors. Yet, as Carnes writes, "The illness concept helps affirm the personal worth of the addict, and such affirmation penetrates the primitive logic of core beliefs, opening the addict to new possibilities."[5] In the context of Twelve Step groups, the

removal of individual responsibility creates the paradoxical result of increasing individual responsibility; and the removal of false shame and guilt feelings paradoxically results in the substitution of healthy remorse and guilt.

Persons who have not suffered from a compulsive illness do not realize the way in which an addiction behaves as an alien will that dominates the addict's native will. For those who have not experienced the Mr. Hyde–like power of an addiction, a special measure of empathy is required in order to minister. Even then, the addict will have difficulty believing that anyone can understand his or her struggle.

But in the context of an anonymous group, many addicts for the first time realize they are not alone, that others have faced the same struggle. The first step of AA reads: "We admitted we were powerless over alcohol—that our lives had become unmanageable." Adapted for sexual addicts, it reads: "We admitted we were powerless over our sexual addiction—that our lives had become unmanageable." In those words, sexual addicts see reflected the truth of their own life. It is a truth that contains both bad news and good news. The bad news is that indeed they are powerless in the face of the addiction. The good news is that because the human struggle for mastery is fruitless, the lifelong wrestling match is over.

Carnes writes:

> Alcoholics Anonymous has known for years that the secret to recovery for the alcoholic and the alcoholic's family members is first to admit they are powerless. Acknowledging loss of the power of choice precedes recovery. Looking at the problem of alcoholism as an illness with a definite symptomology has moved the problem from the moral to the medical. Fortunately, most professionals . . . appreciate the fact that a person regains choice by admitting powerlessness and that values can be reclaimed by moving out of the realm of morality.[6]

The experience of the founders of AA, reflected in the experience of countless addicts since, did not stop at the admission of powerlessness, however. The next steps moved from the experience of powerlessness to reliance on a "Higher Power." In the words of steps two and three: "[We] came to believe that a Power greater than ourselves could restore us to sanity. [We] made a decision to turn our will and our lives over to the care of God, *as we understood Him*." This is essentially the movement from Romans 7 (in which the apostle Paul cries out in despair because of his powerlessness over the sin principle within himself) to Romans 8 (in which Paul describes the freedom that can be experienced when one is led by the indwelling Spirit of God).

Carnes speaks of reclaiming values by moving out of the realm of morality. It may be more proper, theologically, to talk about reclaiming the spirit of holiness by moving out of the realm of the law.

But as all students of the gospel know, no longer living under the law does not mean the abandonment of moral responsibility. The founders of AA discovered that turning themselves over to a Higher Power could not happen without self-examination, confession, restitution, and the experience of forgiveness. Highlights of steps four through nine read: "[We] made a searching . . . moral inventory . . . ; admitted to God . . . and to another human being the exact nature of our wrongs; . . . asked Him to remove our shortcomings; made a list of all persons we had harmed . . . ; made direct amends to such people whenever possible, except when to do so would injure them or others."

The final three steps reflect the classic disciplines of the Christian life: continued self-examination and confession, prayer and meditation, witness, and the integration of these principles in all of life.

Recovery, not respectability

When these principles are seen to be a summary of Christian conversion and sanctification (which they are, although they are often dressed in secular clothing), it is tempting to ask why an addict needs to turn from the church to these groups with their shadowy, anonymous existence. The answer is that most addicts find it impossible to transform their core belief system in the context of most churches. Of course, some have been fortunate enough to find local churches that are not judgmental and moralistic. But most congregations are not able to move beyond lip service to the dictum that "the church is a hospital for sinners rather than a club for saints."

This is how the leader of an ex-gay ministry quoted earlier reports his own experience with the church:

> The Christian churches in dealing with homosexuality tend to settle for control. My own church, when talking about my recovery, tends to speak in terms of my being in control and being careful. They talk as if I am always on the edge. Most of the leaders of ex-gay ministry, I hope, are convinced that that's not recovery.

The role of the church in Anglo-American culture has been to serve as a primary certifier of social respectability. Although the church no longer serves as the conscience of general society as it once did, in many places it still retains its sociological role as a gathering of the respectable. Addicts, however, are not in search of respectability. If anything, respectability may have been too highly valued in their upbringing. Rather, they are very likely in search of intimacy and trust. The relationships that nurture those values are not easily developed in an atmosphere in which "respectability" is so highly prized. Although addicts have indeed found help in the church, it is much more likely that in the company of others of their own experience, guided by gospel principles (whether directly from Scripture or in the form of the Twelve Steps), that they will be able honestly to examine their own pasts and rebuild their core beliefs.

Because addicts need a variety of help, the wise minister will look for a way to coordinate the efforts of church, anonymous group, and therapist in the healing of the homosexual addict. Many ministers are used to being a jack of all trades. It is in the nature of their jobs. But combining the strengths of each source of help will help the addict find freedom.

The addictive process, says Carnes, is "the loss of one personality as it is overcome by a second personality—the addictive personality." "In intervention and treatment," he writes, "addicts recover their true selves."[7] In the context of a team approach to healing, that true self will discover that it can learn to trust, that it can indeed be intimate, that it can both enjoy sex and subordinate it to other values, and that it is of inestimable worth to Jesus Christ.

Notes

1. *Out of the Shadows* (Minneapolis: CompCare, 1985) provides an excellent introduction to the subject of sexual addiction. It is widely available and easy to read. But anyone whose professional commitments bring him or her in contact with people who are acting out sexually, should read *Contrary to Love* (Minneapolis: CompCare, 1988), Carnes's more thorough and technical explanation of sexual addiction and its treatment modalities.

2. Cited in Carnes, *Contrary to Love*, p. 26.

3. The following data are drawn from research reported in *Contrary to Love*, pp. 128 ff.

4. Ibid., pp. 89–90.

5. Ibid., p. 234.

6. Ibid., p. 22.

7. Ibid., p. 46.

Chapter 7

HOMOSEXUALITY ACCORDING TO SCIENCE

Stanton L. Jones

It has happened more than once—a friend has said casually, "Of course, the church's historic stance on homosexuality is totally outmoded in light of what we now know about it." He would go on to say the genetic origins of homosexuality are unquestioned, that mental-health professionals no longer consider homosexuality a psychological or psychiatric disorder, that any amount or type of known intervention cannot change a person's sexual tendencies, and that any position on the part of the church demanding lifelong celibacy or fruitless efforts to change is, of course, inhumane and degrading!

Neither the Christian tradition nor the Scriptures, however, can be responsibly interpreted as approving of homosexual behavior. Because many do argue that recent scientific understandings put the church in a "new hermeneutical situation" where its traditional stance must be altered, we must ask, "What are these new scientific understandings that they speak of?" As a psychologist, I would like to address what the behavioral and social sciences have to say to the church on four key questions: Is homosexuality a psychopathological condition? Is homosexual orientation caused by factors beyond a person's voluntary control? Is change to heterosexuality possible for the homosexual? And, is expression of erotic sexuality essential to wholeness?

Is homosexuality pathological?

This question is central because Christians once took comfort in the secular denunciation of homosexuality as "perverse" and "deviant," which supported their moral condemnation of homosexual behavior. In 1974, however, the American Psychiatric Association (APA) removed homosexuality from the approved list of pathological psychiatric conditions. Many take this action to mean that homosexuality is no longer a psychopathology, a "mental illness." But knowledge of the history and context of the APA's decision suggests that this simple answer will not work. The vote occurred at a time of tremendous social upheaval, at unprecedented speed, and under conditions of explicit threats from the gay-rights movement to disrupt APA conventions and research.

While the deletion of homosexuality from the professionally authoritative *Diagnostic and Statistical Manual of Mental Illness* was in response to a majority vote of the APA, it appears that the majority of the APA membership continued to view homosexuality as pathological. Four years after the vote, a survey found 69 percent of psychiatrists believed that homosexuality "usually represents a pathological adaptation."[1]

Thus the question "Is homosexuality pathological?" is still alive. No absolute standard exists in this area, but four empirical criteria are often used to define abnormality: statistical infrequency, personal distress, maladaptiveness, and deviation from social norms.

As a lifelong, exclusive or near-exclusive orientation, homosexuality is not a common pattern, but neither is it rare. Kinsey found 4 percent of white males to be exclusively homosexual throughout their lives and a total of 10 percent of white males to be mostly or exclusively homosexual during at least a three-year period between the ages of sixteen and fifty-five.[2] Kinsey's data are generally believed to overrepresent male homosexuality because of sampling biases in his research—that is, his survey overrepresents prison inmates, Protestants, the highly educated, and urban dwellers. Other estimates range from 1 percent to 4 percent for exclusive homosexual orientation among males. The incidence among females is commonly reported to be half that of males. (Less research exists on female homosexuality.)

While it is clear that contemporary research cannot be interpreted as saying that one out of ten persons in the general population is homosexual (a common assertion), quibbling about prevalence does not answer the psychopathology question: By what criterion can anyone judge homosexuality as normal at 10 percent and abnormal at 4 percent of the population? There exists no basis for deciding on pathology by mere statistical frequency.

Does homosexuality always and inherently involve personal distress? Most contemporary researchers conclude current standards do not indicate homosexuals as a group are not more emotionally disturbed than are heterosexuals. Yet some researchers have conclusively documented higher rates of depression and loneliness, suicide attempts, and substance abuse in this population.[3] Such elevated levels of distress among homosexuals (e.g., depression or suicidality) are often attributed to the interaction of homosexuals with a rejecting society, not to any discomfort produced by the orientation itself. These responses are likened to those of any persecuted or disenfranchised minority, and there is certainly some validity to such an argument.

The question of the maladaptiveness of homosexuality is difficult because this question can be answered with reference to a number of standards whose results are mixed. Positively, homosexuals have been prominent among those who have contributed to our society and culture: artists, scientists, literary figures, educators, and so on. Homosexuality itself does not seem to prevent a person from being a productive and functional member of society. Note, however, that this point is an argument by association. One could also argue against homosexuality by associating it instead with the perverse acts committed by such individuals as John Gacy. Clearly neither position provides any useful information about adaptiveness.

On another level, the biological adaptiveness of homosexuality was once questioned on the basis that homosexuality does not contribute to the propagation of the species. On the one hand, this view is not often voiced today, given current overpopulation fears. On the other hand, the AIDS epidemic has given pause to many regarding the biological adaptiveness of male homosexuality. The rampant spread of AIDS in the male homosexual population appears to be due to many factors, including several that are endemic to male homosexuality itself. First, anal intercourse almost always involves tearing of rectal tissue and resulting in semen-blood contact (the two fluids containing the highest concentrations of the AIDS virus in the body). Second, promiscuity among many homosexuals has promoted the rapid spread of the virus. Third, some aspects of the stressful gay lifestyle may undermine the body's normal capacity for fighting off infection (including the AIDS virus).

Another area of controversy concerning the adaptiveness of homosexuality involves relational stability. While it appears that lesbians show a capacity to form long-term monogamous relationships in a manner comparable to that of heterosexuals, male homosexuals as a group show a greatly reduced capacity for such relationships and a propensity for promiscuity. The famous Bell and Weinberg study found that only 10 percent of male homosexual respondents in a nonrandom but large sample could be classified as existing in couple relationships characterized as even "relatively monogamous" or "relatively less promiscuous." In the same study, 28 percent of white homosexual males reported having had one thousand or more homosexual partners in their lifetime, only 17 percent reported having had fewer than fifty partners, and 79 percent reported that more than half of their sexual partners were strangers.[4]

Fidelity to and stability within monogamous relationships used to be a prominent feature in definitions of emotional health, but it is rarely emphasized today. If one presupposes that the capacity to form stable monogamous erotic relationships is an essential adaptive capacity, then real difficulties for male homosexuals emerge. If the psychological community deemphasizes relational stability among its criteria of adaptiveness or healthy emotional adjustment, then promiscuity in the male homosexual community does not constitute maladjustment.

Most judgments of the adaptiveness of homosexuality are made according to whether homosexuals achieve what theories of normal human development understand to be wholeness and health. For example, conventional psychodynamically oriented practitioners judge homosexuality as representing a fixation or regression in development. In this model, heterosexuality is presumed to be the natural endpoint of growth as a person; homosexuals do not reach that endpoint, and so their condition is judged maladaptive. Unfortunately, developmental models are always open to dispute—which is why the psychological and psychiatric communities have collectively retreated from using such models to make formal judgments about normalcy.

Finally, does homosexuality violate societal norms? Recent studies of public opinion show that about three-fourths of the general public view all instances of homosexual behavior as immoral.[5] In the case of homosexuality, the mental-health establishment seems to have committed itself to revising rather than reflecting the predominant majority public response—that is, to normalizing behavior clearly rejected by the public.

Determining whether or not homosexuality is inherently pathological is a difficult and unresolved task for behavioral scientists. Homosexuality is infrequent but not rare; it is not inevitably correlated with personal distress; judgments of its maladaptiveness are inconclusive; and it violates societal norms. This mixed scorecard reflects the confusion and disagreement in the field today about the pathological status of homosexuality.

I would not regard homosexuality to be a psychopathology in the same sense as schizophrenia or phobic disorders. But neither can it be viewed as a normal "lifestyle variation" on a par with being introverted versus extroverted. Christians typically believe genital homosexual acts are immoral and that immorality is an abnormal (unintended by God) condition for humanity. It also seems undeniable that a Christian understanding of persons commits one to regarding heterosexuality as the optimal goal of human sexual and relational fulfillment.

Thus, homosexuality must be regarded as a problematic erotic orientation that contemporary social science can help us understand. One can take such a stand without regarding it as a psychopathology *per se*. Such a stance permits one to support the ordination of celibate persons of homosexual orientation who are otherwise suited and called to the ministry, in that homosexual orientation cannot be equated with diagnosing the individual as "neurotic" or "psychotic." Further, designating a behavior as pathological is not necessary for that behavior to be viewed as sin. Idolatry, sorcery, pride, and greed are not recognized pathologies, but they are sins.

Does homosexual orientation develop involuntarily?
This question often reflects the presupposition that God would not declare as sinful proclivities that people had no part in establishing. The major hypothesized causes for homosexual orientation today focus on genetic, prenatal hormonal, and psychological factors.

Early identical-twin research into the causes for homosexuality suggested a strong genetic component, but these results have not been replicated. Today, it is generally concluded that there is some degree of genetic influence in the development of some homosexual persons, but the operative mechanisms are not direct.

The most powerful biological theory of causation today looks at prenatal hormones. Studies introducing abnormal hormone levels in pregnant animals have shown dramatic effects on sexual differentiation and erotic development in offspring. Hormone levels in human fetuses can unquestionably affect physical development, brain functioning, gender orientation, and adult behavior.

Does this suggest a prenatal hormonal cause of all or most homosexuality? While some theorists propose such a model, the evidence is either based on animal research that does not begin to approximate the complexities of the human situation or on correlational human research from which we cannot clearly adduce causation. A number of experts have concluded that prenatal influences may provide a "push" in the direction of homosexuality, but there is as yet no conclusive evidence that this push is powerful enough to be determinative. Further, there is no evidence that this push is present for all homosexuals. Many argue that psychological influences may result in a homosexual orientation without any predisposing prenatal influences.

Postnatal hormonal theories were once common, but the general consensus today is that there are no major differences in hormone levels between heterosexuals and homosexuals. In any case, all but the most extreme hormone variations have little impact on sexual interests and choices in humans.

Psychoanalytic theories of causation are well known. These assert that homosexuality is the result of serious disturbances of family dynamics during childhood. Psychoanalyst Irving Bieber developed the most familiar model: that homosexuality may result from a disturbance in parent-child relationships where a distant father frustrates a boy's need to identify with his father, and a smothering and controlling mother blocks efforts at independent development and maturation.[6] Bieber's theory, based on clinical work and research with nearly one thousand homosexuals, meets with varying responses in the mental-health community, ranging from outright dismissal to total acceptance. Others, including Christian analyst Elizabeth Moberly, offer different psychoanalytic interpretations of homosexuality.[7] While findings are intriguing, the general consensus is that psychoanalysts have not offered conclusive evidence for their theories.

Other psychological theories focus on the role of learning, suggesting that early sexual and other emotional experiences shape erotic orientation. For example, a boy with troubled family relationships and a pre-existing tendency toward effeminate behavior may be more likely to experience his early erotic experiences in a homosexual fashion, begin to define himself as homosexual, and may subsequently choose homosexual interactions even when heterosexual options are available.

One view argues that erotic orientation is typically solidified during adolescence through the interaction of the biological sex drive and experience. In normal social development, boys turn from exclusively same-sex friendships to mixed-gender relationships around the time of puberty, which aids the development of heterosexuality, in that boys have greater exposure to girls at about the same time that the sex-drive begins to blossom in response to the pubescent surge of sex hormones. For some boys, however, precocious onset of sex drive can lead to direction of sexual urges toward other boys.[8] Conclusive evidence for these theories is lacking.

Two final lines of evidence suggest that the causes of homosexuality are not exclusively biological. First, though homosexual behavior occurs often in the animal kingdom, it most often occurs in interactions between dominant and subordinate animals, when other-sex mating partners are unavailable, or under stresses such as crowding. Stable, lifelong homosexual orientation in animals is quite unusual, a pattern one would not expect if genetic or prenatal influences determine homosexual orientation.

Second, homosexual behavior occurs to some extent in all known human cultures, but the form it takes varies, suggesting that the meaning attributed to homosexual behavior in the culture is a prominent influence on the behavior itself. For example, in the Sambia tribe of New Guinea, all males are taken from their families around the age of seven to live communally with the older single men of the tribe. In that company, prepubertal boys are expected to perform oral sex on the postpubertal single men, as they believe that boys can only grow to be men when fed on the "milk of men." When the boys reach puberty, they switch roles to be the ones on whom oral sex is performed. Finally, after they marry, they are expected to function exclusively as heterosexual married men.[9]

In other cultures, homosexual behavior seems to occur for two main reasons: lack of available other-sex partners or as part of a culturally defined ritual. The concept of homosexual orientation as a stable, lifelong pattern does not seem to exist in all societies, and it is rare in preindustrial societies. Therefore, is homosexuality developed involuntarily? This divergent phenomenon appears to be the product of a host of factors, with causes and facilitating influences varying from person to person. Psychological, familial, and cultural influences may be most important. It appears that homosexuality can develop without genetic or hormonal factors, but generally it does not develop without learning and socialization.

The scientific literature often seems to assume that humans are buffeted about by external and internal mechanisms. Such a view of human passivity seems sub-Christian, but a Christian view of persons cannot deny that biological and social forces influence our lives. A Christian view would suggest that we respond to these influences with subtle or obvious responsible acts of our own, adding our own choices to the host of influences that shape our personalities. We may fail to see the impact of our choices because the decisions that shape our lives are often not grand, climactic ones but small, cumulative ones that result in our being kind or cruel, envious or thankful, idolatrous or godly. We cannot, on the basis of scientific evidence, rule out some human accountability for our problematic sexual orientations.

It is possible, on the other hand, that some individuals are the helpless victims of powerful influences that shape their orientation in its original form, particularly in the vulnerable period of childhood. God unquestionably allows some of his children to bear the brunt of powerful external events for which they are not responsible. But in the case of homosexual orientation, we would need to affirm the individual's responsibility for acting on that preference. By analogy, an adult child of an alcoholic may have biological and psychological predispositions to respond positively to alcohol, but he or she must face the responsibility of choosing whether or not to indulge that predisposition. Focusing on why we are the way we are cannot eliminate the question: "How should I act given what and who I am?"

Can homosexuals become heterosexuals?

A textbook I began using recently says unequivocally that psychotherapy for homosexuality "has been ineffective." This is an erroneous conclusion. Change is possible for some. Every study of conversion (from homosexual to heterosexual) reports some successes, ranging from 33 percent to 60 percent. In a curious non sequitur, however, opponents of such therapies use the modest cure rates to argue that no cure is possible.

Change, however, *is* difficult. It does not follow from a simple willingness to change or some straightforward set of procedures. Change is most likely when the counselee is young, highly motivated, has functioned successfully as a heterosexual, does not manifest gender-identity confusion, and has been involved in minimal homosexual behavior. Change of homosexual orientation may sometimes be impossible by any natural means.

A number of Christian groups claim that change is impossible and seek to have Christians accept monogamous homosexuality. But there are also a growing number of Christian ministries attempting to help homosexuals change. These latter groups offer a variety of approaches, but generally they concur that change is a difficult and painful process of renouncing sinful practices and attitudes, and reaching out to grasp God's promise of help. These groups suggest that struggling with homosexual attraction is a lifelong task, but that the person who takes on that struggle can expect gradual change. Some aim at change to heterosexuality; others seek merely to replace compulsive homosexual passions and behavior with an experience of fulfilled chaste singleness. Unfortunately, these groups have not systematically documented their success rates. At this date there is only minimal scientific evidence that change is possible through these means—although there is dramatic anecdotal evidence.

Is expression of erotic sexuality essential to wholeness?
What is to be said to the individual who says, "We have to express our sexuality to be whole people or we are denying our essential humanness. To deny us our sexual expression is inhumane, degrading, and destructive to our growth as persons."

Of the four questions at issue here, practically no direct scientific evidence exists for this question. In our sexually charged society, many claim sexual gratification is fundamental to human happiness; and yet, no empirical research has been conducted on this question. No evidence proves that the sexually abstinent are any more or less disturbed or fulfilled than the sexually active. Each major personality theory in psychology today places sexuality in a different place in a person's life; some place it at a person's core while others place it on a person's periphery. None of the major theories asserts that the expression of genital erotic urges is essential to human well-being. Even Freudian theory, the most "sexualized" of the theories, does not posit genital gratification to be essential to wholeness.

Again, if change to heterosexuality is not forthcoming, is it contrary to a person's well-being to commend abstinence? No basis in behavioral science or Christian theology suggests that abstinence is detrimental to human welfare and that expression of genital eroticism is necessary for wholeness. Although God intended genital expression to occur within marriage, it seems inconceivable that

God would create us with a drive that *must* be expressed for wholeness, put up a wall of rules stifling its expression (except in heterosexual marriage), and then condemn all singles to perpetual frustration. To assert that our sexuality is a force that must be genitally expressed for us to be whole is unacceptable. The homosexual is asked no more and no less than each human being—to follow Christ in submitting his or her natural tendencies to the Father.

A compassionate and pastoral answer

Have recent developments in the behavioral sciences put the church in a "new hermeneutical situation" in which it must revise its understanding of Scripture and tradition? The behavioral sciences do not hold the answers to church deliberations about the morality of homosexual behavior and other related questions, but there is much of value that the church can learn about homosexuality from the behavioral sciences.

While we know much more about homosexuality than ever before, we have not learned anything that mandates a radical overhaul of the historic stance. What we have learned should increase our compassion and pastoral effectiveness. It should also end harsh, simplistic, and judgmental condemnation toward homosexual persons. We must assert that homosexual individuals are not disordered in all aspects of their being; many homosexuals are loving, creative, compassionate people of great wisdom and insight. Homosexual sins are not in a special category meriting our hatred and disgust. To live out the call of the gospel properly, we must faithfully regard as sin all that God himself condemns; we must also embody the character of Christ, who loved sinners and gave his life for them. By his stripes, we must all be healed.

Notes

1. R. Bayer, *Homosexuality and American Psychiatry: The Politics of Diagnosis* (New York: Basic Books, 1981), p. 167.
2. See A. C. Kinsey, W. B. Pomeroy, and C. E. Martin, *Sexual Behavior in the Human Male* (Philadelphia: Saunders Company, 1948).

3. A. P. Bell and M. S. Weinberg, *Homosexualities: A Study of Diversity Among Men & Women* (New York: Simon and Schuster, 1978), pp. 207 and 450.

4. Ibid., pp. 308 and 346.

5. See J. Davis and T. Smith, *General Social Surveys (1972–1984): Cumulative Data* (New Haven, Conn.: Yale University Press, 1984).

6. Irving Bieber, "A Discussion of Homosexuality: The Ethical Challenge," *Journal of Consulting and Clinical Psychology 44*, pp. 163–66.

7. See Elizabeth Moberly, *Psychogenesis: The Early Development of Gender Identity* (London: Routledge and Kegan Paul, 1983).

8. M. Storms, "A Theory of Erotic Orientation Development," *Psychological Review 88*, pp. 340–53.

9. R. Stoller and G. Herdt, "Theories of Origin of Male Homosexuality: A Cross-cultural Look," *Archives of General Psychiatry 42*, pp. 399–404.

Chapter 8

MEDICAL PERSPECTIVE OF THE HOMOSEXUAL ISSUE

Bernard J. Klamecki

For the past twenty-nine years, as a rectal specialist (proctologist), I have treated thousands of people with ano-rectal and colon problems. Homosexuals have accounted for a growing number of these patients: from 1 percent of my practice in 1960 to 25 percent of my practice in 1988. The majority of the homosexual patient referrals were through the Gay Unions Free Clinic and included a large number of cruisers and male prostitutes.

Over the years, as the percentage of homosexuals in my patient load increased, my attitude changed from critical judgment and "you deserve this" to a deep sadness, sympathy, compassion, and love. So often, as I have listened to the patient's story, I would cry out within my spirit, "Lord Jesus, what would you do if you were here? Would you cry out to your Father asking him to pour his love into these men's lives? Teach me how to forgive and be forgiven of my prejudices; how to love and heal as you did."

As I got more in touch with my own prejudices, fears, woundedness, and weakness, I could then get more in touch with the patient's unspoken fears, frustrations, confusion, anguish, and resignation. There seemed to be no hope, no cure. What did I have to offer once the medical treatment had been exhausted? There was and is one answer: Jesus Christ. When prayer for and with the patient is offered, how exciting and humbling it is to see our Lord move in glory, power, healing, and love.

But before I share personal experiences in which I saw God heal the spiritual wounds of homosexuals, I first need to describe the physical afflictions of homosexuals so that both their spiritual and physical needs can be understood. The medical/surgical problems associated with homosexual practices are of a growing concern not only to me, but also to health-care professionals and church people. I know well the medical and surgical pathology directly related to the sexual practices typical of active homosexuals, particularly anal intercourse (sodomy) and oral intercourse (fellatio). Moreover, I have learned from hundreds of cases that unless the emotional and spiritual aspects of a patient are also treated, the ano-rectal, colon, or other organ-systems pathology will persist.

Sexual practices typical of homosexuals can affect the oral cavities, lungs, penis, prostate, bladder, anus, perianal areas outside of the rectum, rectum, colon, vagina, uterus, pelvic area, brain, skin, blood, immune system, and other body systems. The following problems are classified as mechanically induced, chemically induced, and sexually transmitted. While none of the following practices is unique to homosexuals, they are nonetheless typical.

Mechanically induced—pathology induced by force or motion
Male homosexuals engage in a number of sexual practices that could lead to health problems. Most common is anal intercourse (sodomy), whereby the penis is inserted into the recipient's anus. This practice is not limited to male homosexuals but is also performed in heterosexual relationships as a birth control method or variant sexual position. Both the anal receiver or passive partner and the anal inserter or active partner can experience orgasm.

Foreign objects are often used in order to produce a different erotic sensation or to instigate a more violent sexual activity (sadomasochism). Objects that I have removed from the rectum and lower bowel include corn cobs, light bulbs, vibrators, soda bottles, and varied wooden sticks.

"Fisting" is when a fisted hand is inserted into the rectum, sometimes as far as the elbow, which produces varied sexually exciting sensations, strongly linking eroticism with pain. This practice is usually performed while under the influence of LSD, marijuana, cocaine, or nitrites.

Oral intercourse (fellatio) is when the penis is inserted into a recipient's mouth and is therefore not necessarily restricted to homosexuals. The physical problems that result include tearing of the tongue, lining of the mouth and upper throat, and bite marks to the penis.

Rimming (analingus) is when the tongue is used to lick or tickle the outlet of the rectum for sexual excitement, arousing, or foreplay. Needless to say, bacteria may contaminate and infect the mouth. One other sexual practice is "Water Sports," in which urinating into the mouth or rectum is used as a sexual stimulant.

Physical damage to the rectum may occur because of some of these practices. For example, because of the push/pull motion by a fairly hard, almost 1¾- to 2-inch diameter object (whether penis or foreign object) into an opening not designed to receive such an object, damage to the opening and its surrounding structure can occur. There is an antinatural activity being performed when the rectum is the recipient of a penis or foreign object. Because of this activity, cracking of the tissue (fissuring), open sores (ulcers), boils (abscesses), and other infections can occur in the skin of the surrounding tissues.

If rectal penetration is a frequent activity, the recipient's rectal muscles may be injured and weakened, causing poor bowel or gas control. If the activity is violent, as in fisting or the use of large rough foreign objects, the walls of the rectum or lower bowel may be perforated. Persistent anal-rectal sexual activity can lead to various precancerous lesions such as Bowen's disease and Kaposi's sarcoma (see AIDS section). Whenever tissues are traumatized, cracked, or abraded, they are vulnerable to bacterial infection.

Symptoms resulting from the previously described conditions can consist of pain during the actual erotic act or the normal functions of the body, such as pain with a bowel movement, burning with urination, or multiple female-organ pain. Blood and/or a discharge of pus may also accompany the bodily function. Since infections can disrupt normal bodily functions, changes in bowel habits, urination, swallowing, and menstrual periods can occur. Rapid formation of painful lumps can mean boils, tumors, or ulcerated sores. Painless lumps around the outlet of the rectum can be due to enlargement of pre-existing hemorrhoids. Many discharges from the rectum, penis, vagina, or open sores can cause itching and burning rashes, which are due to poor hygiene and infection.

All of the disorders listed so far and most of those yet to be discussed can be treated with good results. Treatment can be divided into conservative (or nonsurgical) and surgical. Abstinence, of course, is the best preventive measure. The source of the trauma or infection must be removed; otherwise, all treatment is futile and the condition will return. That is why strong, loving medical and/or psychological and/or spiritual advice must be given. I have never had a patient react negatively whenever I approach treatment in a wholistic manner—that is, physically, psychologically, and spiritually.

Conservative treatment consists in dietary changes in order to eliminate scratchy foods, spicy and highly acidic foods, and alcoholic beverages in order to produce the least-irritating bowel movements possible. Often, high-fiber supplements are given in order to produce soft bulk. Moist or dry heat is used to soothe painful, irritated areas, reduce swelling, and enforce hygiene. Appropriate antibiotics are used for the infections, and medicated suppositories or ointments are used for the rectal, vaginal, and skin problems that allow for a lessening of the various skin irritations and open sores.

Surgical treatment is used to remove anal fissures or ulcers that do not heal under conservative treatment, lance any boils present, repair damaged walls or rectal muscles, and remove hemorrhoids, tumors, or foreign objects left in the rectum or bowel. Most operations are expensive because of the hospitalization, anesthesia, and surgical abilities involved. Again, if abstinence is practiced, results should be good.

Chemically induced

Up to 86 percent of homosexual males use amyl and butyl nitrite, or poppers. Poppers cause blood to engorge all of the genitourinary blood vessels, giving a heightened "rush" around orgasm while abruptly lowering the blood pressure, and causing dizziness or giddiness and a skin sensitivity that enhances touch pleasure. Dangerous side effects include heart-rhythm problems, fainting from lowered blood pressure, a rapid heart rate, and headache. Also, nitrite vapors are highly flammable.

Other drugs used are alcohol, marijuana, cocaine, hallucinogens, amphetamines, barbiturates, angel dust, and, perhaps, worst of all, IV drugs. All reduce moral resistance and enhance fantasy.

Sexually transmitted diseases

These diseases are associated with anal intercourse, fellatio, and the exchange of body fluids through kissing, licking genitals (cunnilingus on the female and analingus on either sex), and other behaviors. A large percentage of the diseases afflict the bowel, rectum, and urinary system for the following reasons:

1. Homosexuals and bisexuals have more sexual partners than do heterosexuals: 20 percent average 100 per year, with the early AIDS patient averaging close to 1,000 yearly.

2. Group contact with anonymous partners may take place frequently in unhygienic settings, such as back-room bars, health clubs, adult bookstores, and public bathrooms.

3. The lining of the mouth cavity and rectum was not designed to be conducive to the traumatic, ongoing push/pull motion of sodomy or fellatio. In contrast, the lining of the vagina is composed of cells that lubricate themselves and are resistant to the mechanical forces of intercourse. Persistent rubbing easily abrades, breaks down, or injures the tissues of the mouth and rectum.

4. Worldwide sexual activity, as a result of traveling, exposes homosexuals to exotic and unusual organisms.

Bacterial diseases:

Diseases caused by bacteria and other organisms will be discussed in order of frequency. Most of the sexually transmitted diseases are easily treated and cured *if* diagnosed early and treated vigorously with the proper medications, and *if* the infected person takes responsibility to be celibate. AIDS will be treated separately because of its unique behavior and the fact that it is usually terminal.

Gonorrhea (N. gonorrhoeae) has been spreading rapidly during the past several years, especially among promiscuous youth as well as homosexuals. What is alarming is that 80 to 90 percent of all rectal infections have no symptoms. On the other side, 95 percent of all penile infections are symptomatic (usually a discharge). Gonorrhea may easily infect extragenital and rectal sites, such as the mouth, by direct contact according to the sexual practice, or indirectly by spreading through the bloodstream. It is commonly found in the mouth, where it is usually asymptomatic.

In women, gonorrhea is not symptomatic until it spreads into the uterus, fallopian tubes, and out into the ovaries and peritoneum, causing pelvic inflammatory disease. This condition is painful and associated with fever, chills, and general sickness, but it is readily treated with procaine penicillin and Benemid.

Chlamydia is considered to be the most common venereal disease, yet the most undiagnosed, affecting anywhere from three to ten million people. It accounts for 90 percent of the urinary infections in college students and for prostatitis in males under thirty-five. It is the major cause of sterility and infertility in females, due to infection of the lining of the uterus and the fallopian tubes. Inflammation of the rectum is not unusual and usually is asymptomatic. This disease is easily treated with tetracyclines.

Syphilis is a disease that dates back to biblical times; manifestations of this disease have been found in mummies. It is due to an organism called a spirochete *(T. pallidum)* that is contained in the drainage from painless open sores (ulcers or chancres) on the genitals, and it is highly contagious. If not diagnosed and treated, it can be devastating as it attacks the brain, causing neuro-syphilis. To this date, it is part of premarital blood testing, called the VDRL (Venereal Disease Research Laboratories). This disease has various stages, with the chancres, skin problems, warts, and serologic changes being early in the disease. If treated early with penicillin, it is curable.

Amebiasis and *giardiasis*, or traveler's diarrhea, usually cause dysentery (watery bowel movements) and are diagnosed by laboratory studies and easily treated with appropriate antibiotics. *Shigellosis, Campylobacter, Salmonella,* and *Yersinia* all cause watery stools. These diseases, including amebiasis and giardiasis, necessitate the taking of a detailed medical, social, and sexual history. The stools then need to be tested for blood cells, bacteria, parasites, and their eggs, after which the appropriate treatment may be instituted.

Viral diseases:
Viral-induced diseases can be the most difficult to treat—if at all, because of no known treatment, no vaccines, or poor response to treatment. The most common are the Genital Herpes Simplex Virus (HSV), hepatitis A and B, cytomegalovirus, condyloma acuminatum (rectal warts), and AIDS. Of these, the ones I see most commonly are:

Rectal warts, caused by a virus called papovavirus, which primarily enters the center (nucleus) of squamous epithelial tissue cells and replicates, producing warts in the warm, soft, moist tissues of the body. The usual sites are the genitals, anal canal, around the outlet of the rectum, in the urine tract (urethra) of the male or female, and even in the mouth. From time of contact to formation of the warts is anywhere from one month to one year (averaging three months). The warts may be minimal in number, scattered, or in the thousands. They are difficult to treat and have a high recurrence rate.

The patient usually complains of the rapid formation of "hemorrhoids," itching, burning, or any combination of the complaints. Treatment may depend on the number, site, and size of the warts and can be conservative or surgical. Conservative methods include chemical removal, chemotherapy with 5-FU ointment (also used to destroy cancer cells), or vaccine made from the patient's own warts.

Surgical removal or destruction can be by excision (cutting), electrical destruction, freezing, and laser (which is used to cut or burn the warts away). All of the above techniques are futile if the virus remains in the underlying cells. Dehydrating agents, powders, proper rest and diet, vitamin therapy, and other symptomatic treatment may help. This disease is bothersome rather than life-threatening.

Genital Herpes Simplex (HSV) affects more Americans than syphilis and gonorrhea combined. It is easily spread by sexual contact and by self-inoculation, such as touching the genital area and then rubbing one's eyes. All of the recto-vaginal-genital areas are commonly involved. Because it is painful and highly resistant to treatment, it is the source of organic and psychological complications. For example, 25 percent of babies born through an infected birth canal die; 25 percent suffer some brain damage; and 50 percent will be left unharmed.

Symptoms consist of fever, headache, muscle aches, stiff neck, photophobia (in which light causes eye pain), and skin problems. Multiple pustules form, which break and cause painful ulcers in the involved areas. Also, there can be painful urination or vaginal discharge. Treatment is according to the symptoms and with fairly new antiviral agents. Because of the painful areas, sexual abstinence becomes more than voluntary.

Hepatitis, or inflammation of the liver, is classified as Type A or Type B. Type A is passed sexually as well as by contaminated food or a contaminated joint of marijuana. It is easily treated. Type B, however, is much more serious because it is difficult to diagnose and treat. At least three out of four cases have asymptomatic infections or infections that do not reach a level of observable jaundice (yellowing of the eyes and skin) or an enlarged, painful liver. Other symptoms are similar to the other viral infections.

About 200,000 new infections are reported yearly, with 25 percent reaching clinical significance. At least 5,000 patients will die of hepatitis B or related diseases. Between 6 and 10 percent of young adults will become carriers. The treatment is symptomatic, enforced rest, and a hepatitis B vaccine.

AIDS

AIDS, or acquired immune deficiency syndrome, is a disease that has gripped the attention of the entire world. Statistics concerning its increase and global spread bring varied reactions: grave concern, demands for more money for research, and cries that AIDS is God's wrath, the consequence of human sinfulness.

As we read and listen daily to reports about AIDS, HIV (human immunodeficiency virus), or HTLV (human T-cell lymphotrophic virus I, II, or III), we realize that these diseases are complex, perplexing, and mysterious. These diseases are difficult to catch unless one is having promiscuous sex (unprotected), sharing unsterilized IV drug needles, or in some way coming into contact with contaminated blood. About 1.5 million people are currently affected in the United States (according to an article in *Scientific American*, October 1988).

The way AIDS is acquired is when a virus in an infected person's blood, semen, or vaginal fluid enters the body of another through the insertion of the penis, fist, or other object. It enters directly into the blood stream through small (unseen by the naked eye) tears in the lining of the rectum, mouth, or vagina.

In drug users, the virus enters directly into the blood stream through the needle puncture site. Users of IV drugs make up 25 percent of AIDS cases. Infected male and female prostitutes are frequent IV drug abusers. The virus is carried in contaminated blood left in the needle, syringe, or other drug-related objects.

Today, testing makes the receiving of contaminated blood transfusions unlikely. The virus may also be transmitted during pregnancy and breast feeding. AIDS is not transmitted through casual everyday contact, such as touching, sneezing, saliva, bathrooms, toothbrushes, towels, utensils, mosquitos, pets, tears, or school activity.

About 70 percent of AIDS victims in the United States are male homosexuals or bisexuals. No race, culture, religion, economic level, social or educational level, or age group is spared. The risk of infection increases according to the number of sexual partners one has, whether male or female.

The only sign of the AIDS infection may be a positive blood test for antibodies to the virus, with no symptoms for a long period of time or even indefinitely. When the virus enters the blood stream and attacks certain white blood cells called T-lymphocytes (immune system cells), substances called antibodies are then produced by the body, and they try to combat this attack. These antibodies can be detected in the blood by a simple test, usually two weeks to three months after the infection. Even before the antibody test is determined positive, however, the victim can pass the virus to others.

In some people, as the protective immune system is destroyed by the virus, other germs and cancers cause "opportunistic diseases," using the opportunity of lowered resistance to infect and destroy.

Several of the most common of these diseases are Pneumocystis carinii pneumonia and tuberculosis. A common cancer is Kaposi's sarcoma. Such infected people have classic AIDS.

As the virus continues to attack and destroy the immune-system cells, as well as other parts of the body, the body's defense or ability to resist disease weakens. The person becomes more vulnerable to infections and cancers. As the disease progresses, the person becomes overwhelmed by other diseases and eventually dies. Without an immune system, we are susceptible to being infected by bacteria, fungi, other viruses, and malignancies.

Some signs and symptoms of AIDS and the opportunistic infections may include persistent fever and cough associated with shortness of breath and difficulty breathing (carinii pneumonia), multiple purplish blotches and lumps on the skin (Kaposi's sarcoma), and increasing weakness, to the point of being bedridden. The virus can also attack the nervous system and cause damage to the brain.

There is no cure at present, nor is there any type of vaccine. Treatment, therefore, becomes symptomatic, supportive, and eventually comforting. A recent drug, AZT, offers some temporary relief. The disease, however, is at this time ultimately fatal.

A physician's prayer

I write as a medical professional, sharing my experience-based conviction that God is not so interested in our eloquence as in our availability, that he is not so interested in our techniques as in the tithing of our professional time. Having practiced the surgical treatment of rectal diseases over the past twenty-four years, I would like to share two brief experiences that confirm my conviction that the Lord honors prayer and availability.

My first experience with prayer and healing has forever convinced me that God is at his best in our weakness. In 1976, God asked me to be an instrument in a man's conversion. Daniel was a twenty-six-year-old homosexual, whom I treated for venereal warts. He was a warm, gentle, talented, outgoing young man. On the day of his final checkup, Daniel brought a humorous gift for my office wall. It was a framed miniature mink-covered bedpan with an inscription that read: "Nothing is too good for my patients." He then thanked me and said good-bye. The "good-bye" was to be forever, because he was moving to San Francisco to join a homosexual community of professionals.

When Daniel said, "Thank you," I told him that was not necessary as I had only done what I was trained to do: operate and help him to heal.

But he said, "No, you did more than that. In fact, it's for what you didn't do that I am thankful." Somewhat surprised, I asked him just what it was that I did not do. Daniel said, "You didn't judge me."

"Judge you?" I replied. "Why should I have judged you?"

"Well," he said, "When I looked around your waiting room and offices I saw that you are a spiritual man, and therefore I thought you would judge me as other doctors have. But you didn't."

I always have a cross in my waiting room, plus a cross-stitched *shalom*, and a little sign that reads: "The Truest Joy of a Christian Is Knowing that His Life Serves." What Daniel could not have known is that I have dedicated my office to our Lord and asked that he, as Prince of Peace, Savior, Bridegroom, and Divine Physician, be present in my reception room, office, and examining rooms. *And he is!*

My reply to Daniel was, "I am not here to judge but to get people well. There is much I wanted to say to you, but didn't and wouldn't because you never asked. But there is one thing I would like to say to you now if you don't mind. Do you?"

"No," he replied.

"What I would like to say is that your body, emotions, and talents are some of God's greatest gifts to you and to others. And the Giver of gifts desires you to use those gifts in the way they were intended. Especially our bodies. They must not be misused or abused, as they are the holy temple in which he chooses to reside. Please remember this."

"Perhaps someday I will think about it, but now I enjoy my life and sexuality the way they are. If I ever change my mind, I will let you know."

With that Daniel left, and I did not hear from him until many months later when a letter arrived from San Francisco. I did not recognize the name and return address until I started to read it. The letter contained a long description of his life in the homosexual community and what had happened to him. I will summarize his letter:

> I have been leading a very active homosexual life, which was the cause of my getting gonorrhea of the rectum. When I went to the doctor for treatment, he asked me whether I wanted daily antibiotics for ten days or one massive dose by injection. I elected to receive the injection. Within seconds after receiving it, I began to feel light-headed and had difficulty breathing. My heart started to beat rapidly and then all went black. Later the doctor told me I went into anaphylactic shock and died. There was no pulse, heartbeat, and the electrocardiogram was flat.
>
> But here is what happened to me, doctor. After everything went black, I saw myself lying on the floor with the doctors and nurses doing things and seeming very upset. I left the room and went through a long, dark passageway. Just before entering it, my entire life passed before my eyes just like a rapidly spinning carousel. My grandparents came to me. They were the ones who raised me, but died several years ago. There were other relatives who died many years before. They were aware of my homosexual activities, as these events passed by, but not one condemned me or made me feel ashamed. All of them loved me. I could feel their love.
>
> After being in the dark passageway for awhile, I saw light in the distance. It grew larger and brighter as I approached it. Finally, I came out of the black hole and entered into a magnificent garden. As I continued on, I came to a fence which I could not get over, around, or through. It stretched in either direction as far as I could see with no obvious gate. A brilliant light, which came from the other side of the fence, exuded warmth and love and peace, and I knew that it was *The Magnificent One, The Omnipotent One.* I felt drawn to the light, but the fence obstructed my way. I heard a voice come from the light, which said, "It is not time to come into my Father's Kingdom. For the gifts which you have received from me you have not used as I have intended. Go back and use them to glorify me." It was then I woke up in the doctor's

office all wired, everyone running and very excited. The doctor told me I was dead for almost ten minutes. But I am no longer dead, doctor. I am alive! I now know what you wanted to tell me, what you did tell me, and what God wants me to be. Doctor, I have been cured of my homosexuality. I am in a strong, supportive Christian community, which I need as I adjust to my new lifestyle. God has given me a new chance to live according to his plan and not mine. I humbly thank him.

Another experience of God's honoring a simple prayer occurred a short time ago. I walked into my examination room ready to interview a new patient. What I found was a young man, Bill, weeping. I felt startled and embarrassed. Before I could say anything, Bill pointed to a picture on the wall and said, "That picture makes me weep!" The picture was one of Jesus Christ with his hands lifted up and eyes raised in prayer; it was entitled *Father, Who Art in Heaven.*

Before I could speak, he continued, "Doctor, I'm a homosexual, and I don't want to be one. Is it wrong, doctor? Is it harmful? Help me, doctor!" Never had I been asked such questions; never had I sensed such apparent desperation. While he asked these questions, I was praying quietly in the Spirit, something I always do while listening to patients' complaints. When he finished, my first question was, "Why are you here?" The young man stated that he had growths around his rectal outlet that had been increasing in size and number over the past month or so.

"Doctor, please let me tell you when they appeared. Will you listen to me?" Such anguish! He was sitting at the edge of the seat, hands tightly clasped, weeping and pleading to be heard. I nodded, and he began. "I'm twenty-three years old and never had a physical relationship with a man until recently. My home is in California, and my father is a minister. For as long as I can remember, older men have attracted me, but I never had any sexual relationships with them. I enjoyed homosexually oriented magazines, fantasies of sexual activities with men when I masturbated, and I frequented the surfing beaches. These feelings, desires, and needs were getting so strong that I could no longer bear them." As he talked, I felt his agony so intensely that I wanted to cry.

He continued. "I finally decided to speak to my father. So I told him how I felt, what I feared, and asked if he would help me. He listened quietly, never asking a question or making a comment. When I finished, without any expression on his face, he got up, went to the door of his study, opened it, and said, 'Out! You are a disgrace to our family, this church, and to me. Get out and do not come back.' I left and eventually ended up here in Milwaukee and became a prostitute in order to support myself. A patient of yours took me in and supports me, since I am his lover."

After he finished, I told him that I could help him, and not just his rectal problems. While he was getting ready for the examination, I left the room. I felt like weeping. There was such a heaviness in my chest, especially when I thought about his father casting him out while our Father waits for us to come back to his house. As I walked back into the room, I prayed: "Lord Jesus, if you were here, what would you do?"

Once the exam was finished, diagnosis made, treatment and medication prescribed, I said to him, "You asked if homosexuality is wrong and if it is harmful." My answer is yes to both of your questions. I believe you know it to be so, because you said you did not want to be a homosexual. But you must also know that our Heavenly Father loves you as his son; he does not hate you, reject you, or abandon you. There is an emotional and spiritual illness along with the physical pathology. I will treat your body. What I would also like to do is say a prayer with you, asking the Father to heal all of you."

"Do something, doctor," he replied. "Please do something." His anguish and desire reminded me of the woman with a hemorrhage in the Gospel who struggled to touch the hem of our Lord's garment.

We joined hands across the examination table, and I prayed: "Father, we praise and thank you for this day, asking that Bill be healed in the name of your Son, Jesus. He knows something is wrong. He has physical, emotional, and spiritual pain. So please heal him and bring your love into his entire being, especially all those areas in his past that are so unloved. May Jesus' risen human sexuality bring the needed balance into his sexuality, masculinity, emotions, sexual desires, and responses, wherever or however it is needed. Free him, Father. In Jesus' name, we take complete authority over Bill and ask you to wash him in your Son's most precious blood. Thank you for already having heard our prayer, Father. May you be glorified, Amen."

Bill was crushing my hands and sobbing uncontrollably. He let out a huge sigh that made me think he was going to faint. I went around the table and held him as he cried. When he stopped, he looked at me and said, "I felt the arms of the Father around me."

Regardless of what fatherly love and affirmation are missing during boyhood and adolescence, I have found that the heavenly Father's love can pour into those needy areas of the past and bring new life and direction. In this context the Scripture passage that says "There is no father but the heavenly Father" has become especially meaningful to me.

Bill returned six times for continued treatment and prayer. He began to read Scripture and pray, and he joined a nondenominational church. His sexual partner noticed the change and told him not to come to my office anymore. One day Bill came in and announced to my receptionist nurse, "I'm going to lead a celibate life!" He meant that he was going to move out into his own apartment. Beginning to weep, Bill told me how much he loved his former partner and would miss him. I told him that it was all right to do so. That man had taken him in, fed him, clothed him, sent him to the university, and loved him in the only way he knew how, but now there was a *new love* in Bill's life. Our final prayer included praying for that former partner, that his mind would come into accordance with that of Jesus Christ, so that the will of the Father would be done in and through him.

Reflecting upon these two men and my experiences with them, I realized God honors simple prayers, even prayers uttered within the constraints of professional time. As a physician, I never know what problems I will come up against when I walk into my consultation room. There is a fairly rigid schedule to be followed; only so much time is allotted to each patient. Thus there is not nearly the opportunity for me to listen and dialogue as there would be if I were a therapist, counselor, or pastor. Yet, I believe that within the professional time available to me with each patient, God honors the tithing of my time. He honors my simple prayers and my desire to be his healer of the spiritual and emotional as well as of the physical.

Jesus Christ blesses my saying yes to his invitation to heal broken bodies and spirits, regardless of how inadequate or weak I feel. My prayer experiences have taught me that if I rely upon him, his using me to do his will to love and heal his people, then the right words will come, along with his fruits and gifts. It is in this way—simple, honest availability—that his kingdom comes and his will is done on earth as it is in heaven.

Chapter 9

WHAT DOES THE OLD TESTAMENT SAY ABOUT HOMOSEXUALITY?

Ronald M. Springett

T he biblical issues concerning homosexuality are numerous and complex. These issues arise partly because of the various views about the inspiration and authority of Scripture that are currently held in the theological world. Presuppositions and world views that conflict with traditional scriptural interpretation and that influence biblical scholars also contribute to the complexity of these issues. Some of these scholars settle ahead of time what the Scriptures can or cannot say about homosexuality or any other subject. Others are completely hostile to the Bible's self-understanding.

Once the biblical documents are forbidden to speak for themselves and are forced to say what the present mentality says they must say, the outcome is predictable. Many modern scholars restrict the interpretation of the past to what is acceptable in the present. The result is that many modern interpretations of biblical history bear some resemblance to the Whig interpretation of history critiqued by Butterfield:

> If we turn our present into an absolute to which all other generations are merely relative, we are in any case losing the truer vision of ourselves which history is able to give; we fail to realize those things in which we too are merely relative, and we lose a chance of discovering where, in the stream of the centuries, we ourselves, and our ideas and prejudices stand.[1]

As in Whig historical interpretation, so in much secular analysis of Scripture, the present generation cannot see where it stands in history. Instead of being looked upon as just another part of the historical process, the present outlook has been used as the standard for judging all biblical history.

In a chapter of this length it would be impossible to analyze adequately the current theological impact on the Bible, and perhaps not even desirable for the present purposes. With respect to homosexuality, however, just a brief review of the major issues raised may be useful. At the top of the list is the outright rejection of the inspiration and authority of the Bible. The Scriptures are looked upon as merely human writings. They are not seen to express the mind of God and are no more authoritative than anyone else's "word."[2] In this view, the Scriptures are personal opinions comparable to any other personal opinion. Much more subtle is the inference that the Scriptures lack the benefit of "scientific" insight and the results of biblical scholarship, and therefore are not to be cited as authority in questions of modern ethics and morals.

This argument tends to surface under two basic headings: The first of these suggests that the Scriptures are not really relevant for today. The ancient texts did not condemn homosexuality itself. It was only condemned because of its association with idolatry; that is, because pagans engaged in homosexuality during their worship of other gods, it had a cultic or symbolic significance that it does not have now.[3] To cite Scripture today against homosexuality, outside the context of idolatry, is seen as irrelevant and highly misleading.

In the second line of thought, the Scriptures are irrelevant because the authors were time conditioned and ignorant of distinctions that modern society makes between the "invert" and the "pervert." The invert, on the one hand, is someone who has the "natural" condition of homosexual (or same-sex) attraction; the pervert does not. So, for the invert to engage in homosexual acts is morally and ethically right as long as it is in a loving and responsible relationship. This is his or her "natural" sexual outlet. The pervert, on the other hand, whose natural inclination is toward the opposite sex, is engaging in perversion if he or she consorts with the same sex. It is claimed that the biblical authors knew nothing about the "condition" of homosexuality or the modern invert. Consequently, in the Scriptures, homosexuality is condemned as rape, perversion, or exploitation. The loving relationship between two constitutional homosexuals is not really condemned because natural homosexual attraction was not known in biblical times, or at least not understood.[4]

At this point, two important views of homosexuality need to be surveyed with reference to the Bible: The Bible opposes homosexuality, or the Bible does not oppose homosexuality. Here we present a condensation of material by New Testament scholar Robin Scroggs[5] concerning the pros and cons.

First, the positions that articulate the Bible's opposition to homosexuality. Notice that even in places where the Scriptures are seen to oppose homosexuality, Scroggs's presuppositions seem to invalidate the authority of Scripture in two out of four following cases:

1. The Bible opposes homosexuality and is definitive for what the church should think and do about it. Here the Bible stands as the objective revelation of God's eternal will. God is completely opposed to homosexuality.

2. The Bible opposes homosexuality, but it is just one sin among many. There is no justification for singling it out as more serious than other sins castigated in the Bible. Here homosexuality is a sin, but not a unique sin, and no worse than that of liars, thieves, or drunkards.

3. The Bible opposes homosexuality, but specific injunctions must be placed in the larger biblical context of the theology of

creation, sin, judgment, and grace. Here we have essentially the "analogy of faith" argument. It goes something like this: The heart of the Bible is its central message. This central message is used as a principle to evaluate other less-specific or less-essential parts of Scripture. The actual application of this principle can take many directions since the interpreter decides what is central. Homosexuality will, therefore, be viewed in different lights depending on the central principle: for example, creation, love, and justification.

4. The Bible opposes homosexuality but is so time- and culture-bound that its injunctions may be and should be discarded if other considerations suggest better alternatives. Here contemporary biological, psychological, theological, or sociological considerations may outweigh the biblical material (as authority) in forming a judgment about homosexuality.

Second, Scroggs's summary of positions that claim the Bible does not oppose homosexuality:[6]

1. The Bible does not oppose homosexuality because it does not speak of true or innate homosexuality but rather of homosexual acts by people who are not homosexuals. This is basically the "invert" versus "pervert" argument.

2. The Bible does not oppose homosexuality because the texts do not deal with homosexuality in general. Here the key phrase is "in general." The Bible opposes prostitution and idolatry in conjunction with homosexuality, not homosexuality as such. Whenever the Bible appears to condemn homosexuality, it is related evils that are really being condemned, not homosexuality.

Pertinent questions that we must ask of Scroggs are: What is meant by homosexuality? Is the Bible opposed to a predisposition to same-sex attraction or homosexual acts or both? Is God opposed to any individual who has a homosexual orientation? If not, under what circumstances is it true that God is "completely opposed to homosexuality?" The answers to these and other questions may become clear by a study of the texts.

Key passages in the Old Testament with reference to homosexuality: Sodom (Gen. 19:4-11) and Gibeah (Judg. 19:22-25)
Both of these references have been interpreted throughout the history of the church as attempted homosexual assault. In the Genesis account, some have even claimed that homosexuality caused Sodom's destruction. It was not until D. Sherwin Bailey presented the first extensive and radically new interpretation of this passage that traditional interpretations have been questioned.[7]

In this new interpretation of the Sodom account, the idea that the inhabitants of that city were given to homosexual practices is dismissed for lack of evidence. The question is asked: "What ground is there for the persistent belief that the inhabitants of the city were addicted to male homosexual practices and were punished accordingly?"[8] In this view, there is no ground at all in Genesis 19:5 for such a conclusion.

— In the passage "bring them out to us that we may know them," the word *know* is interpreted as meaning nothing more than "get acquainted with." The whole idea of sexual assault, according to this view, is read into the text. This conclusion, it is suggested, is backed up by lexical statistics. The word *know—yadha—*occurs some 943 times in the Old Testament, but in only twelve instances, without qualification, does it mean coitus. On the basis of these statistics, there is no actual necessity to interpret "know" in Genesis 19:5 as having sexual connotations.[9] Few biblical scholars, however, agree with this restricted interpretation of *yadha*.[10]

One detail that does not help the new view is the fact that verse 8 clearly contains a reference to *yadha* meaning coitus, "I have two daughters who have not known man; let me bring them out to you and do to them as you please." Even if Lot were unpopular, as this interpretation suggests, and even if he were a resident alien who had brought strangers into his house against the local custom, this act still seems radical. If, as Bailey[11] claims, the citizens simply wanted to become "acquainted" with Lot's visitors, why the violence? If the crowd were made up of concerned citizens who wanted to clarify the status of Lot's visitors, why would Lot offer his daughters to them? Lot's offer of his daughters, according to this new view, is incongruous and would have heightened the suspicions of the citizens about the visitors. If *know* in verse 5 simply means "get acquainted with,"

Lot grossly misunderstood the citizens. His best course of action would have been to acquaint them with the visitors.

The Gibeah incident recorded in Judges 19 is similar to the Sodom account in Genesis 19. A man who is a resident alien in an Israelite city protects his guest, a stranger, from a violent rabble. In this account, two women are also offered and one is sent out. She is raped and abused all night and finally dies. This crime is the immediate cause of a war between the tribes of Israel and the tribe of Benjamin, which has dire consequences for the latter.

Many commentators from a higher criticism perspective assume that one of the authors of these similar accounts had heard about, or was looking at, the other author's work. The Sodom story is usually considered the older. In that case, we may have here a commentary on the sin of Sodom. Here also the demand is made to "know" the guest. "Bring out the man who came into your house, that we may know him." Again, according to the new view, it is insisted that even here the word *yadha* simply means "get acquainted with" despite the text, which concerns the Levites' concubine, stating "they knew [*yadha*] her, and abused her all night until the morning."

As in the case of the Sodom story, the traditional view that the Gibeathites were prone to homosexual practices and desired the Levite for the satisfaction of their unnatural lusts is said to be nothing more than an inference from the words: "Bring forth the man . . . that we may know him"—the verb *yadha*, "to know," being erroneously construed in a coital sense.[12]

Now if we had, in both texts, only the first ambiguous reference to "know" (*yadha*), there would be a much better case for the new view. With the offer of the women in Genesis and the second unambiguous use of the word *know* in Judges, however, the ambiguity of the first use of the word disappears. The remark of the host who implores the Gibeathites not to do this "foolish" thing also supports this interpretation. Cundall[13] observes that the use of the word *foolish* (*nebalah*) denotes "an insensibility to the claims of God or man. . . ." Better translations would be *impiety* or *wantonness*, implying that these men were not about to recognize any moral or religious claims upon them.

Bailey is aware of the thrust and import of *nebalah* but brushes it aside as an editorial addition introduced to bring this story into line with the Sodom account. He suggests it is nothing more than "a rhetorical addition designed to emphasize the deplorable lack of courtesy shown by the Gibeathites towards the visitor."[14] Currie sees *nebalah* as a technical term involving a violation of covenant obligations. "But all uses thus listed clearly point at violation of covenant obligations to the LORD and especially to wanton sexual conduct out of keeping with allegiance to YHWH."[15]

Bailey's interpretations have been extremely influential and are repeated in much of the prohomophile literature (favoring homosexual activity among males) despite the fact that most biblical commentators do not agree with him. Most scholars consider his interpretation to be ingenious but unconvincing since it fails to do justice to the immediate context. Likewise, his interpretation does not fit the wider context provided by the biblical narration nor place the same gravity on these situations that the ancient writers themselves sensed. Consequently, Bartlett's criticism seems fair enough:

> It takes special imaginative power to believe, as Bailey does, that what the men of the city of Gibeah were after was the acquaintance of the visiting man, or that the old man of Gibeah offered his virgin daughter and the other's concubine only to protect his rights of hospitality.[16]

As in Genesis 19, so also in Judges 19, it would be a gross oversimplification to say that *the* sin of those cities was homosexuality alone. The wrongdoing of the Gibeathites, as of the inhabitants of Sodom, included far more than homosexuality. However, in our view, one goes too far when one claims that the Sodomites and Gibeathites had no proclivity to homosexuality. In these passages there is clear reference to attempted homosexual rape, actual heterosexual gang rape, and murder. We cannot agree with Bailey that these accounts merely refer to a gentlemanly disagreement and inhospitality. Both the texts and the contexts suggest far more than that.

Those homophile scholars who concede that the new interpretation is very weak still point out that it is clearly violent homosexual rape that is depicted and condemned in these texts. They say these passages do not speak negatively about a loving homosexual relation between two consenting adults. Therefore, these references cannot be used to condemn such. This may be argued, but there are other biblical references that are not necessarily concerned with rape or violence.

The Holiness Laws:
Idolatry, homosexuality, or both? (Lev. 18:22; 20:13)

These texts clearly prohibit and condemn male homosexual genital activity, but a number of arguments are put forth that attempt to negate their impact. Some see these Levitical laws as part of a cultic taboo in primitive Judaism. Homosexuality is condemned because of its association with the religious practices and licentious behavior of the gentile idolaters. Others assert that these laws applied only to priests, and none of them apply to Christians since the early church had been released from the necessity of keeping these laws.[17]

The Levitical laws, however, need to be seen in the context of Leviticus, chapters 18–20, to be properly appreciated. In the first place, they were not merely for the priests but for the people of Israel (Lev. 15:1–2). Israel should live according to God's laws in order to show the contemporary Near Eastern nations the true nature of holiness, with Israel's priest having a special responsibility. "Not merely are the priests to observe the cultic regulations for ceremonial holiness, but they are required to live lives of moral purity and spiritual dedication, so that they will be examples to Israel of divine holiness."[18] Chapters 18–20 deal with various laws and punishments. In 18, various sexual relationships are predominant—incest, adultery, and homosexuality, as well as child sacrifice and bestiality. Few Christians would be prepared to say that all of these activities are now allowed because the early church was freed from the Levitical law, or that, if it is a loving relationship it is not to be condemned.

But what about such regulations as in Leviticus 19:19? "[Y]ou shall not sow your fields with two kinds of seed; nor shall there come upon you a garment of cloth made of two kinds of stuff." Surely this places these laws in the cultic category. But that is not necessarily so. We have already pointed out that Leviticus contains a mix of cultic and moral regulations. As the covenant people of God, the Israelites were expected to maintain ceremonial and moral holiness.

Homosexuality is condemned because it violates the integrity of creation. As to seeds and cloth, to throw out all of chapters 18 and 19 on the basis of this one verse is surely throwing out the baby with the bath water. Leviticus 19:18 reads, "[Y]ou shall love your neighbor as yourself. . . ." Jesus certainly did not apply the "all-or-nothing" principle in relation to the Levitical laws. Consequently, the great majority of Christians have always recognized the continual ethical and moral significance of much of the material in Exodus 20–40 and Leviticus. The practices listed in chapter 18 have been considered particularly abhorrent to Christians throughout the ages. In addition, the New Testament reiterates the negative stance toward homosexual acts found in Leviticus. This endorsement by the New Testament is perhaps the best criterion we have at present that any particular part of the Levitical law is still an element of God's will for his people.

As noted earlier, the most common argument put forward to negate the Leviticus statements is that homosexuality is only condemned because of its involvement with idolatry. In these verses, it is suggested, a person is condemned as an idolater, not as a homosexual. The unstated assumption is that a person who is a homosexual but not an idolater will not be condemned. John Boswell,[19] professor at Yale University and a key defender of homosexuality, presents a detailed study of the Hebrew word *toevah* and the corresponding Greek *bdelygma* and arrives at this conclusion: The Hebrew word *toevah*, "abomination," in Leviticus 18:22 and 20:13 does not signify something intrinsically evil, such as rape or theft, but something that is ritually unclean. Another point frequently emphasized is that the prohibition of homosexual acts follows immediately upon a prohibition of idolatrous sexuality. So we have in Leviticus 18:21: "And thou shall not let any of thy seed pass through the fire to Molech . . . (KJV)." The implication here is that the Molech text and the text following on homosexuality are both ritual in nature, not ethical or moral.

Although both chapters 18 and 20 contain prohibitions against incest and adultery, advocates of the idolatry thesis contend that their function in this context seems to be as symbols of Jewish distinctiveness. For persons who argue this position, what appears to favor their argument is the claim that the Septuagint, a Greek translation of the Hebrew Scriptures, draws a distinction between intrinsic wrong and ritual purity by translating *toevah* sometimes as *anomia*—that is, violations of law and justice—and sometimes as *bdelygma*—that is, infringements of ritual purity or monotheistic worship. In the Septuagint, homosexuality is characterized as *bdelygma* in both texts.

The conclusion to be drawn from Boswell's argument, it would seem, is that homosexuality was not considered a violation of law and justice and was not itself intrinsically wrong but rather was a matter of ritual purity and monotheistic worship—that is, simply idolatrous. It was something related to Jewish cult and culture but not something immoral or unethical. This argument is quite subtle, but it contains the same sort of logic as Bailey's statistical reasoning concerning *yadha*, "know."

In our view, it is true that in the majority of instances *toevah* does refer to ritual infringements of the law. But just as *yadha* is sometimes used in a sexual sense meaning coitus, so *toevah* is occasionally used in an ethical-moral sense concerning truth and justice (Deut. 25:16; Prov. 8:7; 16:12; 29:27; Jer. 6:15).[20] Although there is a tendency in the Septuagint to ethicize *toevah*, as do the prophets and Proverbs, the Septuagint is not consistent in its treatment of *toevah*. Deuteronomy 25:16, a clearly ethical statement, is described as *bdelygma* in the Septuagint. It should be kept in mind that fundamental to the concept of *bdelygma* in the Septuagint is the fact that God has a contrary mind to this practice and rejects it.[21]

Furthermore, the ancients were not in the habit of neatly dividing their thought and action into the modern categories of sacred and secular. For Jew and pagan alike, the sacred covered all of life, as the Books of Leviticus and Deuteronomy testify. This does not mean that every idea and activity of their pagan neighbors was banned for Jews. Many aspects of the cult and literature of Israel and its neighbors were very similar, with Israel clearly the borrower. It is not enough, therefore, to state that homosexuality was condemned merely because it was a product of pagan society and a part of pagan cult. The reasons why Israel borrowed ideas and practices from its pagan neighbors, which it did, were more complex than this simple formula suggests.[22] Consequently, when Israel did not borrow or even forbade the assimilation of pagan thought and practice, the reasons were likewise more complex than simply the abhorrence of idolatry.

Separation from pagans involved more than just avoiding idolatry. Israel mediated the presence of the divine to its neighbors.[23] The outward form of Israel's religious life was not a matter of indifference (as it almost always was for pagan religion). The visible community was to be clearly distinguishable from the surrounding nations, their multiplicity of gods, and their immoral practices. The fact that these two elements (homosexuality and idolatry) were found together in pagan religion does not mean that they amounted to one and the same thing in Israelite thinking. In our texts we have simple prohibition against homosexual acts. That those acts were sometimes practiced in pagan (idolatrous) rituals also simply compounded the abomination in Israelite thought.

Some Old Testament commentaries,[24] however, agree with Boswell in maintaining that idolatry was the basic problem in these verses. Snaith arrives at a merely cultic ban on homosexuality by interpreting 18:22 in the light of the previous verse (18:21, devoting children to Molech). He observes that the expression *by fire* is not in the Hebrew text. This law, then, is not dealing with child sacrifice by fire to Molech. Rather, it really prohibits giving children to Molech as temple prostitutes. He then connects verses 21 and 22 as both reflecting cultic sexual violation. Homosexuality is condemned because of its association with idolatry.

There are a number of problems with this interpretation. First of all, it would be easier to argue that verse 21 concerning Molech is the verse that is out of context since all other salient verses clearly refer to sexual practices while this one does not. Second, Noth[25] speaks of the Molech law as "striking," suggesting that "it was only the key word 'seed' (RSV, *children*) that brought this verse into the present context." Third, the verse does not necessarily have to mean devotion to Molech either as a prostitute or a sacrifice but may mean that the child was dedicated to the cult as Samuel was to the Israelite temple.

Sapp[26] concludes that the laws against bestiality and homosexuality were based on three major concerns; first of all, that such relations were "simply unnatural." "Moral law and natural law—both products of the one God—could not conflict. Thus to defy nature's law is to violate the revealed law of morality. What nature abhors the law prohibits." Second, and integrally related to the first, is the concern for wasted seed. Finally, the Israelites did see a link between these types of sexual misconduct and idolatry.

The plain meaning of Leviticus 18:22 and 20:13 is a prohibition against male genital homosexual acts. Since no provisional or exception clauses are included, as is the case with some laws, we can only conclude that this is a general prohibition and condemnation of such acts. At least the burden of proof is on those who would interpret these texts to mean something else.

Here, by way of summary, we enter a few caveats concerning the interpretations of the authors already named. Worth mentioning is Bailey's attempt to restrict the interpretation of *know* in Genesis and Judges to one particular meaning of the word regardless of the context. This approach has not been accepted by the majority of scholars, not even by some who agree with Bailey's view of homosexual freedom.

A similar statistical-lexical method is used by Boswell in an attempt to shift the weight of the prohibitions in Leviticus 18:22 and 20:13, from prohibitions against homosexuality itself to a prohibition against idolatrous homosexuality alone. This method also involves sticking to one meaning of a word regardless of the context or significance of the wider passage under consideration. This approach also has a tendency to ignore the inconsistencies in the Septuagint translation of the Hebrew *toevah* and to oversimplify the relations of Israel with her neighbors in the phrase *avoidance of idolatry*. Both Bailey's inhospitality rather than homosexuality (Genesis and Judges) and Boswell's idolatry rather than homosexuality (Leviticus) seem to be read into the respective passages rather than out of them.

Israelite law condemned idolatry. It also condemned homosexuality, and the two were not confused. There is not even a hint that Jesus considered the Levitical laws concerning homosexuality inapplicable to his followers. If anything, the evidence leans in the other direction as it does with the apostle Paul, whom we shall consider in the next chapter.

Notes

1. H. Butterfield, *The Whig Interpretation of History* (New York: Norton, 1965), p. 63. Of course the same result is obtained with a transparent biblicism, which takes neither time nor context into account, but transfers the biblical material point for point across the board into modern situations; for example, the equating of theocratic Israel with Republican America. See S. S. Hill and D. E. Owen, *The New Religious Political Right in America* (Nashville: Abingdon, 1982), p. 44.

2. R. L. Treese, "Homosexuality, a Contemporary View of Biblical Perspectives," *Loving Women/Loving Men, Gay Liberation and the Church*, ed./author S. Gearheart (San Francisco: Glide Publications, 1974), p. 28. Also T. Maurer, "Toward a Theology of Homosexuality— Tried and Found Trite and Tragic," *Is Gay Good? Ethics, Theology and Homosexuality*, ed. W. D. Oberholtzer (Philadelphia: Westminster Press, 1971), pp. 98–100.

3. H. K. Jones, *Toward a Christian Understanding of the Homosexual* (New York: Associated Press, 1966), p. 69.

4. R. Woods, *Another Kind of Love, Homosexuality and Spirituality* (Chicago: Thomas More Press, 1977), p. 103. Also J. J. McNeill, *The Church and the Homosexual* (Kansas City: Sheed, Andrews and McMeel, 1976), p. 39. Also J. B. Nelson, "Religious and Moral Issues in Working with Homosexual Clients," *Homosexuality and Psychotherapy, A Practitioner's Handbook of Affirmative Models*, Journal of Homosexuality, vol. 7, nos. 2/3, ed. J. C. Gonsiorek (New York: Haworth Press, 1982), pp. 166–67.

5. R. Scroggs, *The New Testament and Homosexuality, Contextual Background for Contemporary Debate* (Philadelphia: Fortress Press, 1983), pp. 7–11.

6. Ibid., pp. 11–16.

7. D. S. Bailey, *Homosexuality and the Western Christian Tradition* (Hamden, Conn.: Shoestring Press, 1975). Reprint of 1955 edition.

8. Ibid., p. 1.

9. G. A. Barton, "Sodomy," *Encyclopedia of Religion and Ethics*, ed. J. Hastings (New York: T. & T. Clark, 1928), p. 672.

10. J. P. Lewis, "Yadha," *Theological Wordbook of the Old Testament I*, ed. R. L. Harris (Chicago: Moody Bible Institute, 1981), pp.

366–67; also D. Kidner, *Genesis, an Introduction and Commentary* (Downers Grove, Ill.: InterVarsity Press, 1973), p. 52, are among many who disagree with this interpretation. Even McNeill (a Catholic priest), who advocates responsible homosexual behavior, admits that the case has been overstated here. McNeill, p. 47.

11. Bailey, p. 6. Bailey suggests that Lot offered his daughters because "it was simply the most tempting bribe that Lot could offer on the spur of the moment to appease the hostile crowd."

12. Ibid., p. 55.

13. A. E. Cundall, *Judges, Introduction and Commentary* (Downers Grove, Ill.: InterVarsity Press, 1973), pp. 196–97.

14. Bailey, p. 55.

15. S. D. Currie, "Biblical Studies for a Seminar on Sexuality and the Human Community," *Austin Seminary Bulletin*, 87, 1971, p. 19. Collins also sees human sexuality in the Old Testament as lying in the sphere of human responsibility—a sphere in which humanity has dominion, but within covenant obligations to Yahweh. R. Collins, "The Bible and Sexuality," *Biblical Theology Bulletin*, 7, 1977, p. 158.

16. D. L. Bartlett, "A Biblical Perspective on Homosexuality," *Homosexuality and the Christian Faith, a Symposium*, ed., H. L. Twiss (Valley Forge, Pa.: Judson Press, 1978), p. 25. Wright comments, "Not one critical commentator that I have been able to find takes the position of Bailey and McNeill as summarized by Boswell, that Sodom was destroyed 'not for sexual immorality but for the sin of inhospitality to strangers' (Boswell, p. 94)." J. R. Wright, "Boswell on Homosexuality: A Case Undemonstrated," *Anglican Theological Review*, 66, 1984, pp. 82–83.

17. M. Olson, "Untangling the Web: A Look at What Scripture Does and Does Not Say About Homosexual Behaviour," *The Other Side*, April 1984, p. 25.

18. R. K. Harrison, *Leviticus, an Introduction and Commentary* (Downers Grove, Ill.: InterVarsity Press, 1980), p. 27. See also G. J. Wenham, *The Book of Leviticus* (Grand Rapids: Eerdmans, 1979), p. 3. Most of the laws apply to all Israel; only a few sections specifically concern the priests alone.

19. J. Boswell, *Christianity, Social Tolerance and Homosexuality, Gay People in Western Europe from the Beginning of the Christian Era*

to the Fourteenth Century (Chicago: University of Chicago Press, 1981), pp. 100–01.

20. See F. Brown, S. R. Driver, and C. A. Briggs, *A Hebrew and English Lexicon of the Old Testament* (Oxford: Clarendon Press, 1976), pp. 1072—73, who list Leviticus 19:22 as ethical; see also R. F. Youngblood, "tr'bh to 'eba," *Theological Wordbook of the Old Testament 2*, ed. R. L. Harris (Chicago: Moody Bible Institute, 1981), pp. 976—77.

21. W. Foerster, "bdelyssomai, bdelyktos, bdelygma," *Theological Dictionary of the New Testament I*, ed. G. Kittel, trans. G. W. Bromiley (Grand Rapids: Eerdmans, 1968), pp. 598–99; also, P. M. Ukleja, "Homosexuality and the Old Testament," *Bibliotheca Sacra*, 140, 1983, pp. 262–64.

22. J. Jensen, "The Relevance of the Old Testament, I. A Different Methodological Approach," *Dimensions of Human Sexuality*, ed. D. Doherty (Garden City, N.Y.: Doubleday, 1979), p. 5. As Jensen notes, so frequently did Israel borrow from pagan neighbors that where some objection is raised to a pagan rite, "some reason other than its pagan associations must be sought."

23. W. Eichrodt, *Theology of the Old Testament I* (Philadelphia: Westminster Press, 1967), p. 404. Concerning the testimony of the prophets, Carol Stuhlmueller concludes that "sexual sins like adultery and prostitution, whether involving Gentile or Israelite people, are condemned as evil in se [themselves] and not simply as Canaanite fertility rites which invaded Israelite sanctuaries." C. Stuhlmueller, "The Relevance of the Old Testament, II. Prophetic Ideals and Sexual Morality," *Dimensions of Human Sexuality*, ed. D. Doherty (Garden City, N.Y.: Doubleday, 1979).

24. S. H. Kellog, "The Book of Leviticus," *The Expositor's Bible I*, ed. W. R. Nicoll (Grand Rapids: Eerdmans, 1943), p. 334; N. H. Snaith, *Leviticus and Numbers* (Greenwood, S.C.: Attic Press, 1977), pp. 125–26.

25. M. Noth, *Leviticus, a Commentary*, trans. J. E. Anderson (Philadelphia: Westminster Press, 1965), p. 136.

26. S. Sapp, *Sexuality, the Bible and Science* (Philadelphia: Fortress Press, 1977), p. 31.

Chapter 10

WHAT DOES THE NEW TESTAMENT SAY ABOUT HOMOSEXUALITY?

Ronald M. Springett

I n the previous chapter we discussed the Old Testament accounts concerning homosexuality. In this chapter we will examine Pauline texts that specifically touch the issue of homosexuality.

The form and context of antihomosexual statements in the New Testament.
The early church did not discourage social interaction with those outside the Christian faith, but a clear line was drawn between the ethical-moral behavior expected of those outside, and that expected of those inside, the group (1 Cor. 5:9-13). Paul also discouraged any activity that might involve participation in a cult (1 Cor. 8 and 10). It is clear from the advice given in 1 Corinthians 5 and 6 that Paul

considered the Christian community a pure and holy place as against the impure and profane world outside. Christians were to avoid the abhorrent sexual practices and other vices that the pagans delighted in. In Ephesians 4:17ff., Paul reminds believers what is expected of Christian communities (cf. Col. 3:12ff.). These regulations were essential to the solidarity and cohesiveness of the Christian community as a whole (1 Cor. 1:2). They also highlight Paul's conviction that the purity of the community "is contaminated only from within, not by contact with outsiders, even though the latter are considered typically immoral."[1]

Regulations for Christian ethical behavior were also stated negatively in the early church. This was achieved by listing the vices that Christians were exhorted to avoid. Dodd[2] suggests that such lists may have been used in catechetical instruction from a very early period in the church. Moreover, the Stoic strain in them is unmistakable. The cataloging of virtues and vices into lists was a practice familiar in classical, Hellenistic, and early Christian literature.[3] That is not to say Paul took his ideas directly from the teachings of the great classical schools of philosophy. Rather, as Judge[4] finds, Paul did not have much in common with any regular system of school of thought, but with "the way in which a loose body of general principles for life develops among thoughtful people in a community."[5]

Christians also found negative ethical lists in the Hellenistic Jewish literature. They are abundant in Philo, and an excellent example of a vice list is found in Wisdom 14:25–26: "Blood and murder, theft and fraud, corruption, faithlessness, tumult, perjury, troubling of good, unthankfulness for benefits, defilement of souls, confusion of sex, disorder in marriage, adultery and wantonness." Easton[6] observes that in accord with Jewish custom, actions rather than thoughts are enumerated here; whereas a Stoic list would center on sins of disposition. Also characteristically Jewish is the emphasis on "idolatry" in Wisdom as the cardinal defect, where Greek and Roman (Stoic) moralists would choose "ignorance."[7]

Paul's line of thought in Romans 1:26–31 follows, but does not repeat, much of Wisdom's thesis and language. Of the fifteen terms in Wisdom and the twenty-one in Romans, only two, murder and deceit, are common to both lists.[8] Easton[9] finds non-Jewish precedent highly likely for Romans 1:29–31 and only less likely for

2 Timothy 3:2–4. McEleney[10] finds no pattern of terms followed in the vice lists of the pastoral epistles. He concludes:

> Thus the vice lists of the Pastorals have been influenced by more or less of these elements: (1) reference to the Decalogue or other commands of the Law; (2) polemic against immoral pagan idolaters; (3) Hellenistic conceptions of virtue and vice as qualifications of a man; (4) moral dualism due to various inclinations of spirits in a man causing him to walk in one of two ways; (5) the theme of eschatological punishment.

Here again the Stoic and Jewish backgrounds stand out. The similarities with Stoicism, however, should not be overemphasized. The pagan concept of *philanthropia* (love for humanity), although present in Wisdom, is notably absent in the New Testament. The Christian idea of *makrothymia*, "patience" (Gal. 5:22), is, on the other hand, absent in Stoicism, and such qualities as *eleos*, "mercy," and *tapeinotes*, "humility," are virtues in Christianity and vices in Stoicism. Different views of people, their nature, and purpose in life determine the differences among them. Therefore, it is vital to understand the world view in which the terms are used in the New Testament. As Easton[11] again notes, "[A]voidance of the sins cataloged in these lists is never identified with Christian morality. Life as a Christian hardly begins until such temptations have been put to death." It is highly significant, therefore, that all major references to homosexuality in the New Testament occur in vice lists.

Inverts or perverts or both? (Rom. 1:26–28)

The above verses are followed immediately by the longest vice list (vv. 29–32) in the New Testament. It contains no sexual sins; Paul apparently was satisfied with his treatment of this aspect in verses 24–28, the whole of which (vv. 24–32) may be seen as an extended vice list.

Numerous interpretations of this passage see homosexual acts as being condemned in it. Other interpretations find only a certain kind of exploitative homosexual practice condemned. By far the most prevalent view among the latter is that which sees Paul opposed to homosexual lust and not homosexual acts. This passage, it is claimed, could not be written against the "natural," or permanent or constitutional, homosexual because Paul was ignorant of the distinction between the primary or constitutional homosexual and other, perverted forms of homosexual activity.[12] He is concerned here with exploitation, prostitution, and unbridled homosexual lust. In fact, some would claim, he must be talking, if anything, about those who are not permanent homosexuals, because the text states that those involved in the activity do so "against [their] nature." It would not be against the nature of a constitutional homosexual to indulge in homosexual activity, but it would be against the nature of a heterosexual to do so. This interpretation sees the passage as speaking about perverted heterosexuals who indulge in homosexual acts "for kicks." It does not refer to a loving homosexual relationship of two constitutional homosexuals.[13]

In this discussion the center of attention is focused on the word *nature*. Some interpreters avoid the idea that Paul's use of the word is tied to Greek philosophical usage in some way.[14] Others read it as simply meaning convention, the generally accepted practice in a particular time and place. Among this latter group, 1 Corinthians 11:14 is frequently quoted, "Does not nature itself teach you that for a man to wear long hair is degrading to him." Here Paul uses the word *nature* in what is considered a conventional sense. In the Greco-Roman culture, it was generally accepted practice to have short hair and be close shaven. However, among the Jews, long hair and cropped or uncropped beards were not considered unconventional. Thus, *nature* here seems to mean the nature of the situation in a particular time and place. The implication seems clear according to this line of reasoning: that homosexual acts Paul says are "against nature" are simply not accepted in some societies but are in others; and this is what he means here.[15]

In Romans 1, Paul is showing how far humanity has fallen from the ideal state it once enjoyed. In verse 24, he uses the words "God gave them up." He allows the wicked to "enjoy forever the horrible freedom they have demanded and [they] are, therefore, self-enslaved."[16] True, sin is exposed, and to some extent punished, by its own results, but this is because God has so constituted a natural process in which wrong inevitably gravitates to wretchedness. God leaves people where they place themselves—in the fatal region of self-will and self-indulgence.[17] "There is a moral law in life that men are left to the consequences of their own freely chosen course of action; and unless this tendency is reversed by divine grace, their situation will go from bad to worse."[18]

In verse 26, Paul specifies what results from and contributes to the fallen existence common to men and women. God gives them up to the dishonorable passions that spring from their attitude toward God. Paul mentions homosexuality as a dishonorable passion. That men and women believe they serve God by indulging in these passions is part of the ultimate irony in idolatry—the ultimate foolishness of those who claim to be wise (v. 19). Paul begins with women who exchange natural relations for unnatural. The meaning of this brief verse is made clearer by the next (v. 27). The men likewise gave up natural relations with women and were consumed with passion for one another; men committing shameless acts with men. As already noted, the two key terms in these verses are the expressions *natural* and *unnatural,* and much depends upon what Paul meant here. The crux of the issue concerns the sources on which Paul was ultimately dependent for his judgment that homosexuality is unnatural.

Paul uses the terms *para physin* (against, beside, or contrary to nature) and *kata physin* (according to nature). These Greek words are used to express an ethical judgment on homosexuality. This is true of Plato (*Laws* I, 636; VIII, 841), who uses the terms *natural* (of heterosexual intercourse) and *unnatural* (of homosexual intercourse) numerous times. Plato explains why it is unnatural, saying men cannot fall below the level of the animal world where homosexuality does not take place (*Laws* VIII, 841). These are also common expressions in the Hellenistic period, as we see in Diodorus Siculus (c. 49 B.C.). In his *History* 32, 10, 8–11, he uses the term *kata physin* of natural intercourse with a woman. In this case, however, where the woman was in reality a man, he speaks of the intercourse as having taken place "as with a man" and the marriage as "against nature" (*para physin gamoy*). In any event, the woman (actually a man) had to submit to "unnatural embraces," *para physin homilian.*

Dionysius of Halicarnassus (c. 30 B.C.), in his *Roman Antiquities* XVI, 4, 2–3, speaks of a coercive attempt at homosexuality as *para physin tois arresin hybreis,* "doing violence to the male's natural instincts."

Musonius Rufus, a Roman (Stoic) philosopher sometimes referred to as the Roman Socrates, was a contemporary (c. A.D. 30–101, 102) of Paul whose works show "the typical characteristics of the popularized philosophical treatise.[19] For Musonius, life in accordance with nature is life in accordance with virtue. Musonius identifies *kata physin zen*, "to live according to nature," with *en arete zen*, "to live according to virtue." Men and women may have equal virtue and should have equal training. Not surprisingly, Musonius sees marriage as *kata physin*. In the later Stoics, marriage is always said to be *kata physin*.[20] In fr. XII[21], which is on sexual relationships, he refers to pederasty (a system in which boys provide homosexual favors to their male mentors) as "an outrage against nature," *para physin tolmema*.

Another contemporary of Paul, the Jewish annalist Josephus (c. A.D. 37–97) speaks of sodomy as "unnatural vice," *para physin*, and "unnatural pleasure," *para physin*.[22] It would not be helpful to continue repeating numerous examples of vices spoken of as *para* or *kata physin* from Plutarch and other Hellenistic writers. It might be easier to determine what Paul did *not* mean by this expression and to examine the ideas that separate him from the late Stoics who also used the terms *para physin* and *kata physin*.

Paul's God is transcendent, completely above and beyond the world. God is also creator of nature, but separate from the natural world. The Stoics believed God was immanent, as did Paul, but in ways with which Paul could not agree. For them, not only is the world controlled by God, in the final analysis it *is* God, and therefore basically deterministic.[23]

It is clear Paul uses Stoic philosophical terms in Romans 1 and 2. But it is equally clear Paul does not simply repeat the terms and concepts of Stoic philosophy with the same meanings they had in the Stoic system or even in popular Hellenistic philosophy.[24] That Paul intended by the word *nature* "the providential ordering of the world," as did the Stoics, is probably correct.[25] Apart from this agreement, however, the term has a completely different function for Paul. The meaning of the term in Romans comes from a Stoic-Jewish storehouse.[26]

In other words, Paul's God was not nature, but the supremely transcendent One, above, beyond, and separate from nature. The

Creator formed the earth and made humanity in perfection, which work was subsequently blighted by the entrance of sin. Consequently, for Paul, nature does not determine a person's essence. Within fallen nature, only relative distinctions beween the natural and the unnatural can be made. For the Christian, this fallen natural life is preliminary to life with Christ, and it is validated as natural only because Christ himself entered into this natural life through the Incarnation. Bonhoeffer comments that:

> Through the fall the "creature" becomes "nature." The direct dependence of the creature on God is replaced by the relative freedom of natural life. Within this freedom there are differences between the true and the mistaken use of freedom, and there is, therefore, the difference between the natural and the unnatural. In other words, there is relative openness and relative closedness for Christ.[27]

The natural, from this point of view, is the form of life preserved by God in this fallen world. It is that life that is directed toward justification, redemption, and renewal through Christ. Reason itself is embedded in the natural and is nothing more than the conscious perception of the world as it presents itself to humanity. Thus reason, after the Fall, has not ceased to be reason, but is now fallen.[28]

> From this there follows a conclusion that is of crucial importance, namely, that the natural can never be something that is determined by any single part of any single authority within the fallen world. What is natural cannot be determined by any arbitrary decision, and indeed whatever is set up in this arbitrary manner by an individual, a society or an institution will necessarily collapse and destroy itself in the encounter with the natural which is already established. Whoever does injury to the natural will suffer for it.[29]

In this sense the natural, even as the form of life preserved by God after the Fall, is a given. In the midst of the fallen world, it reflects the splendor of the glory of God's creation and points forward to the restitution of all things.

But Paul's perspective in the passage under consideration is not limited to the relative distinctions between natural and unnatural in the fallen world. Only God's original intention for men and women can be considered determinative for their essence, and this is revealed in his will in Scripture. It is difficult to see what else Paul could mean by *nature* in our text if not the world and humanity as intended and created by God; the *unnatural* being a consequence of the Fall and, therefore, not God's intention and will for men and women. The cosmic sweep of the context of Romans 1:18–32 is generally recognized. Scroggs[30] suggests that in these verses the universal Fall is narrated for both Jews and Gentiles. Thus, homosexuality is not treated merely as an expression of cultic idolatry; rather, both sins are traced back to the bad exchange that men and women have made in departing from the Creator's design and intention.[31]

> In writing about "natural relations," Paul is not referring to individual men and women as they are. His canvas is much broader. He is taking the argument back, far more radically, to man and woman as God created them. By "unnatural" he means "unnatural to mankind in God's creation pattern." And that pattern he clearly understands to be heterosexual. So the distinction between pervert and invert (which Paul could have hardly made anyway) is undercut.[32]

In this light, Paul has in mind not only the casual and capricious sex swapping of the pervert driven by lust and desire for fleshly stimulation, but the basic divergence from God's original creation scheme that all homosexual behavior represents. The invert or constitutional homosexual may be seen as an aberration of God's original creation. And, therefore, he or she is certainly depraved (as we all are to some extent) in the theological sense.[33]

In verse 27, Paul observes that those who practice such acts "receive in their persons the due penalty for their error." The apostle may be speaking of spiritual moral erosion in life, the physical deterioration that results from a dissolute life, or both. At the end of the vice list in verse 32, he further notes "they not only do them but approve those who practice them." Although this applies to the whole vice list, it also serves as a reminder that, in Paul's day, homosexual relationships not only went uncondemned but were sometimes glorified as a plane of love higher than that between man and woman.[34] If homosexual practices could be approved in any sense, surely Paul would have noted that fact and drawn the distinction.[35] But in the absence of such provisos we must conclude that there is no "Pauline privilege" for homosexual activity in Romans 1:26–28.

Homosexuals or prostitutes? (1 Cor. 6:9–10; 1 Tim. 1:8–10)

In his first epistle to the Corinthians, written from Ephesus about A.D. 57, Paul attempts to correct a number of abuses in the church. He had to deal with factions in the church (1:10–4:21), with moral abuses (5:1–6:20), and, in the last part of the epistle, with various questions and problems raised by the members. Our passage falls within the section in 6:1–11 where Paul is remonstrating with the Corinthians about litigation before pagan courts. Paul sees this love of litigation about trivial matters as a survival from a wretched past that all Corinthians ought to have left behind them.

Clearly using the vice list format, Paul begins to enumerate other evils that should belong to the past experience of any Christian. In this list he enumerates ten kinds of offenders. Of the first five, four are sins against purity, including fornicators or immoral persons, adulterers, male prostitutes, and homosexual offenders.

Homosexuals is the translation of two Greek words, *malakoi* and *arsenokoitai*. The translation and meaning of these words are vigorously debated. The primary meaning of *malakos*[36] is "soft." The word is used to describe fabrics (Matt. 11:8; Luke 7:25) or skin, and many other items. It can be used of persons in the sense of "soft of nature," "delicate," or "tender." In a more derogatory sense, the word means "effeminate" or "voluptuous."[37] Moffat[38] translates the words separately as *catamite* and *sodomite* (*catamite* is usually defined as a boy used for pederasty). Other translators see no connection with homosexual acts at all and suggest that the word means loose, morally weak, or lacking in self-control.[39] These translations are usually picked up by prohomophile writers.

The vast majority of commentators[40] and lexicographers of the New Testament, however, see this as a reference to passive homosexuals, to those who yield themselves to be used for homosexual purposes. Some quote papyrus Hibeh 54, "And send us also Zeno-

bius the effeminate with tabret, and cymbals, and rattles. ..."
Malakos here means "effeminate." On this papyrus, Deissmann[41]
comments, "The word is no doubt used in its secondary (obscene)
sense as by St. Paul in 1 Cor. VI, 9. It is an allusion to the foul
practices by which the musician eked out his earnings." The fact
that *malakoi* are mentioned between two other sexual sins in our
text lends weight to the argument that "softness" is not merely self-
indulgence, but as the lexicographers Arndt and Gingrich[42] suggest,
males who allowed themselves to be used homosexually.

The other word, translated *sodomites* by the Jerusalem Bible and
Moffat, is *arsenokoitai*. It is used only in 1 Timothy 1:10 outside our
reference. Some argue that the word refers only to homosexual
prostitutes. Boswell, representing others, argues that the compound
word *arsenokoitai* simply means males involved in sexual activity,
not those who have sex with males.[43] He stresses the coarseness and
active licentiousness of the word, connoting thrusting activeness,
denoting a male who has sex. Hence, he concludes, it is not necessarily a reference to homosexuals at all.[44] This word is first found in the
Palatine Anthology IX, 686, and the verb form is in the Sibylline
Oracles II, 73.[45] Boswell contends that the word is rare in Greek
literature and that it is, therefore, difficult to compare references as
to its usage. Consequently, there are no guidelines in Greek literature that might help to determine whether the first element of the
word "male" is the subject or the object of the last element *koitai* (a
cognate to the English word *coitus*) suggesting "sexual relations."

He also makes a distinction between the *arreno* and *arseno* compounds. *Arreno* compounds, he believes, are employed objectively.
Arreno, "male," being the object of *koitai*, "bed" or "sex," one who
has sex with males, males being the object of sex. This compound is a
reference to homosexual relations. But the compound found in the
Scriptures, *arseno-koitai*, is different, he thinks: a male (subject) who
has sex—the object not specified here. He concludes that it cannot
be demonstrated that any of these New Testament uses of the word
are objective or, therefore, that they imply homosexuality.

Wright,[46] however, in a thorough study on *arsenokoitai*, shows
that Boswell's presentation contains numerous flaws. First of all, he
does not pay sufficient attention to *arsen* and *koite* in the Septuagint
of Leviticus 18:22; 20:13. Second, he does not take into account the

fact that the *arreno, arseno* compounds are dialectical variations, and there is no evidence of any semantic difference between them. Third, there is no lexical evidence for the active, male thrusting connotation that he attaches to the compound *arseno-koitai*. Fourth, there are many more occurrences of the word in Hellenistic literature than Boswell allows that do disclose the meaning it bore for the writers in question. Wright discusses these references in detail and concludes that in 1 Corinthians and 1 Timothy, male prostitution (with females) is out of the question as the meaning of the word, and what is intended is male homosexual activity with youths or adults.

Scroggs notes, correctly in our opinion, that the first element of the word *male* is the object of the action implied in the last part of the Greek word for *sexual relation*. The *arsenokoites*, he concludes, is the active partner in the homosexual relation, while the word *malakos* points to the effeminate call boy who acts as a mistress. Scroggs, however, would not see here a reference to general homosexual practices, but only to homosexual prostitution of the kind indulged in by Timarchus, who was hired or kept by a number of adults, with the usual jealousies and quarrels—a model not aspired to by the gay community today.[47]

Although many commentators agree with Scroggs's exegesis, not all agree with his interpretation of it. If Paul was condemning only one kind of homosexual activity here, and by implication allowing others, he surely would have been more explicit. Coming as he did from a Jewish background and tradition, Paul knew his readers would understand him against that background. If Paul was, as seems to be suggested, flying in the face of Jewish teaching, he could have and would have made himself much clearer. Conzelmann, in his comment on this passage, rightly points out that "the Jewish verdict on the latter [homosexuality] is unequivocal."[48] Is Paul here making a clear and single-handed departure from the traditional Jewish interpretation of Scripture by removing the taint of immorality from *mishkav zakur*? On the basis of the evidence provided, this is to be seriously doubted.

Conclusion

From this brief review of a few texts of Scripture, a number of observations may be made concerning homosexuality as viewed in the Bible. Perhaps the first thing to take note of is that all the texts considered speak about homosexual acts. None of them refers to thoughts, dispositions, or intentions alone. Homosexual acts, whatever the intention, are looked upon in Scripture as, at best, misguided or misdirected emotions and, in the worst light, as a sign of rebellion against God's created design for the sexes. Both are evidence of the perversion that has affected humanity since the Fall, which resulted in alienation from God.

In this and the previous chapter we have examined some of the recent attempts to reconstruct, revise, and reinterpret the texts. The views of Bailey and Boswell figure prominently because they have pioneered in the area of reinterpretation of Scripture and the revision of church history. The thesis of both authors is that the negative attitude of Christians toward homosexual activity is not really based in Scripture nor the tradition of the early church. But neither Bailey nor Boswell—nor anyone else to our knowledge—has done the requisite spade work.

Throughout its history, the church has often spoken to the theology of sex, but with its primary focus on heterosexuality. Bailey and Boswell have raised many questions on the issue of homosexuality that deserve serious answers. In response, scholars in various parts of the Christian community are forging a biblical teaching on human sexuality that will meet the needs and answer the questions of this century.

In the area of the New Testament, words have been restricted to one fixed meaning that favors homosexual expression but does not do justice to the context. Or the vocabulary is redefined so that it produces the required interpretation, again at the expense of contextual integrity. Thus, attempts to construe *nature* in Romans 1 as mere convention—that is, local mores—or to see it as an attempt on Paul's part to make a distinction between acceptable and unacceptable homosexual practice do not ring true to the contextual framework in which these terms are embedded. The wider scope of Pauline and New Testament anthropology are, for the most part, also ignored.

The only occurrences of the word *homosexual* in some versions of the Bible appear in 1 Corinthians and 1 Timothy. It is not surprising, therefore, that those who argue for homosexual expression expend considerable effort in an attempt to revise the meaning of the underlying Greek words. But the attempts to reduce *malakos* to "general looseness" are unconvincing. This is especially the case when the word appears in a vice list and in the midst of a grouping of sexual sins. The word subjected to the longest and most detailed revision is *arsenokoitai*. In an appendix of some fifty-three pages, Boswell attempts to dismantle the meaning of the word as previously and currently understood. The argument suffers from many weaknesses, which have been identified in this chapter.

Perhaps the greatest fault in the presentations of Bailey, Boswell, and others who repeat their arguments, is that they seem to have overlooked almost two millennia of Christian thought and interpretation on these texts. J. R. Wright, who takes Boswell to task, particularly for neglect of patristic evidence, also points out that he "has not been inclined either to investigate or to engage their arguments but instead has produced his own interpretation that indeed fits his central contention but is not at all, at least not yet, accepted in the world of serious biblical scholarship."[49]

Finally, it needs to be stated that the Christian position on the subject does not stand or fall with the fate of a few negative statements about homosexuality. The Bible has much positive material on human sexuality that must be integrated with the negative statements to produce a balanced picture. For instance, Paul describes the beautiful relationship between husbands and wives when he portrays the relationship between Christ and the church. This also must be taken into consideration by those who would claim that homosexual acts are condoned in Scripture.[50]

Notes

1. W. A. Meeks, *The First Urban Christians, the Social World of the Apostle Paul* (New Haven: Yale University Press, 1983), p. 105.

2. C. H. Dodd, "The Ethics of the New Testament," *Moral Principles of Action—Man's Ethical Imperative*, ed. R. N. Anshen (New York: Harper Bros., 1952), pp. 544–45.

3. E. N. O'Neal, "De Cupiditate Divitiarium (Maralia 523c–528b)" *Plutarch's Ethical Writings and Early Christian Literature*, ed. H. D.

Betz. *Studia ad Corpus Hellenisticum Novi Testamenti, Volume 4*, eds., H. D. Betz, G. Delling, W. C. Van Unnik (Leiden, Netherlands: E. J. Brill), 1978, p. 309.

4. E. A. Judge, "St. Paul and Classical Society," *Jahrbuch für Antike und Christentum*, 15, 1972, p. 32. The extent to which the philosophical vice lists had penetrated the popular consciousness may be seen in A. Deissmann, *Light from the Ancient East, the New Testament Illustrated by Recently Discovered Texts of the Graeco-Roman World*, trans. L. R. M. Strachan (New York: Doran, 1927), pp. 314–17.

5. Ibid., p. 33.

6. B. S. Easton, "New Testament Ethical Lists," *Journal of Biblical Literature*, 51, 1932, p. 2.

7. Marcus Aurelius, *Meditationes II*, 1. "Say to thyself at daybreak: I shall come across the busy-body, the thankless, the overbearing, the treacherous, the envious, the unneighborly, all this has befallen them because they know not good from evil."

8. Easton, p. 3.

9. Ibid., p. 8.

10. N. J. McEleney, "The Vice Lists of the Pastoral Epistles," *Catholic Biblical Quarterly*, 36, 1974, p. 218.

11. Easton, p. 8.

12. D. S. Bailey, *Homosexuality and the Western Christian Tradition* (Hamden, Conn.: Shoestring Press, 1975), pp. 38–157.

13. H. K. Jones, *Toward a Christian Understanding of the Homosexual* (New York: Associated Press, 1966), p. 70; R. Woods, *Another Kind of Love, Homosexuality and Spirituality* (Chicago: Thomas More Press, 1977), pp. 104–06; R. L. Treese, "Homosexuality, a Contemporary View of Biblical Perspectives," *Loving Women/Loving Men, Gay Liberation and the Church*, ed./author S. Gearheart (San Francisco: Glide Publications, 1974), p. 38; J. Boswell, *Christianity, Social Tolerance and Homosexuality, Gay People in Western Europe from the Beginning of the Christian Era to the Fourteenth Century* (Chicago: University of Chicago Press, 1981), pp. 110–11; R. W. Wood, "Homosexual Behavior in the Bible," Homophile Studies: *One Institute Quarterly*, Winter, 1962, p. 16; N. Pittenger, *Time for Consent, A Christian's Approach to Homosexuality* (London: SCM Press, 1976), p. 82; D. L. Bartlett, "A Biblical Perspective on Homosexuality,"

Homosexuality and the Christian Faith, a Symposium, ed., H. L. Twiss (Valley Forge, Pa.: Judson Press, 1978), pp. 30–31; Wright points out, however, that no fewer than twenty-two recent critical commentaries fail to make the distinctions on which Boswell bases his interpretation. Most of them generally reinforce the opposite point of view. J. R. Wright, "Boswell on Homosexuality: A Case Undemonstrated," *Anglican Theological Review*, 66, 1984, pp. 86–87.

14. It is particularly Plato's view that homosexuality was "unnatural" because animals did not do it. Scanzoni and Mollenkott take pains to point out that sea gulls and other creatures display lesbian and homosexual behavior. L. Scanzoni and V. R. Mollenkott, *Is the Homosexual My Neighbor?* (New York: Harper & Row, 1978), p. 65. See also Plato, *Laws* VII, 836–40.

15. Boswell, pp. 110–11; also T. D. Perry, *The Lord Is My Shepherd and He Knows I'm Gay* (Los Angeles: Nash Publishing, 1972), p. 152. According to Scroggs, all that can be gathered from this text is that Paul opposes homosexuality. Paul gives no reason. His Greek sources who opposed it likewise gave no reason. Paul's judgment here is ultimately dependent on Greek sources, not Jewish. It is not based on the doctrine of Creation or philosophical principles, but on what appears to be a common-sense observation. See R. Scroggs, *The New Testament and Homosexuality, Contextual Background for Contemporary Debate* (Philadelphia: Fortress Press, 1983), pp. 116–17.

16. C. S. Lewis, *The Problem of Pain* (New York: Macmillan, 1961), pp. 115ff.

17. H. C. G. Moule, *The Epistle to Romans* (London: Pickering and Inglis, 1925), p. 49.

18. F. F. Bruce, *The Epistle of Paul to the Romans: An Introduction and Commentary* (London: Tyndale Press, 1969), p. 86.

19. A. C. Geytenbeck, *Musonius Rufus and Greek Diatribe*, trans. B. L. Hijmans, Jr. (Assen, Netherlands: Van Gorcum, 1963), p. 13.

20. Ibid., p. 68.

21. Fr. XII, 8–10. The Greek text with translation and introduction is found in C. E. Lutz, *Musonius Rufus, "The Roman Socrates"* (New Haven: Yale University Press, 1947).

22. Josephus, *Against Apion*, II, 273, 275; further references may be found in H. Köster, *physis, physikos, physikōs* in *Theological Dictionary of the New Testament IX*, ed. G. Friedrich, trans. G. W.

Bromiley (Grand Rapids: Eerdmans, 1977), pp. 251–77.

23. C. S. Lewis, *Studies in Words* (Cambridge: Cambridge University Press, 1975), p. 41. See the whole chapter on *Physis*. Also, Marcus Aurelius, *Meditationes* IX, 1; Diogenes Laertius, *Lives of Eminent Philosophers*, VII, 139, 142–43, 148; Cicero, *Of the Nature of the Gods*, I, 14–15. On Stoic determinism, see E. Bevan, *Stoics and Skeptics* (New York: Arno Press, 1979).

24. A. J. Malherbe, "The Apologetic Theology of the Preaching of Peter," *Restoration Quarterly*, 13, 1970, p. 211. Paul does not share the ideal underlying the Stoic terms, "because for him there is no nature either detached from God or identifiable with God." Also, E. Käsemann, *Commentary on Romans*, trans. ed., G. W. Bromiley (Grand Rapids: Eerdmans, 1980), p. 48.

25. A. J. Herschbell, "De Virtute Morale (Moralia 523c–528b)," *Plutarch's Ethical Writings and Early Christian Literature*, ed., H. D. Betz, *Studia ad Corpus Hellenisticum Novi Testamenti*, Vol. 4, eds., H. D. Betz, G. Delling, W. C. Van Unnik (Leiden, Netherlands: E. J. Brill, 1978), p. 167. Also, Köster, p. 273. For the Stoics, to be in conformity with nature was to be in harmony with God. For Paul, this would not necessarily be so, for nature, too, was fallen. Even for the Stoics, what was natural for animals was not necessarily natural for humanity. See Bevan, pp. 55, 60, 61.

26. C. H. Dodd, *The Epistle of Paul to the Romans* (London: Harper & Row, 1932), pp. xxxii, 26–27.

27. D. Bonhoeffer, *Ethics*, ed. E. Bethge (New York: Macmillan, 1968), p. 145.

28. Ibid., p. 146.

29. Ibid., p. 147.

30. Scroggs, p. 110.

31. D. H. Field, "Homosexuality," *The Illustrated Bible Dictionary* 2, ed. J. D. Douglas (Wheaton, Ill.: Tyndale House, 1980), p. 657. Also Köster, p. 266.

32. D. H. Field, *The Homosexual Way—A Christian Option?* (Downers Grove, Ill.: InterVarsity Press, 1979), 1980, p. 6. On this point see also D. Atkinson, *Homosexuals in the Christian Fellowship* (Grand Rapids: Eerdmans, 1979), pp. 87–88; P. Coleman, *Christian Attitudes to Homosexuality* (London: SPCK, 1980), p. 90. Coleman sees a strong relation to the Noachian Law, p. 93; R. F. Lovelace,

Homosexuality and the Church (Old Tappan, N.J.: Fleming H. Revell, 1978), p. 92; E. A. Malloy, *Homosexuality and the Christian Way of Life* (Washington D.C.: University Press of America, 1981), p. 194; J. Murray, *The Epistle to the Romans, the English Text with Introduction, Exposition and Notes* (Grand Rapids: Eerdmans, 1971), pp. 47–48; E. Brunner, *The Divine Imperative*, trans. O. Wyon (Philadelphia: Westminster Press, 1947), p. 282; G. L. Bahnsen, *Homosexuality: A Biblical View* (Grand Rapids: Baker Books, 1979), p. 50; C. E. B. Cranfield, *A Critical and Exegetical Commentary on the Epistle to the Romans*, 2 Vols. (Edinburgh: T & T Clark, 1975), Vol. I, pp. 125–26.

33. H. Thielicke, *The Ethics of Sex*, trans. J. W. Doberstein (Greenwood, S.C.: Attic Press, 1978), p. 282.

34. E. Best, *The Letter of Paul to the Romans* (Cambridge: Cambridge University Press, 1967), p. 23; Lovelace, p. 92.

35. Bahnsen (*Homosexuality: A Biblical View*) shows that Paul is able to draw fine distinctions at other places in his epistles. We cannot entirely agree with Furnish when he says, "To Paul it represented a rebellion against the Creator and his creation, a surrender to one's lusts, and the debasement of one's own true identity and the exploitation of another's. It is no longer possible to share Paul's belief that homosexual conduct always and necessarily involves all these things." V. P. Furnish, *The Moral Teaching of Paul* (Nashville: Abingdon, 1979), p. 81.

36. H. G. Liddell and R. Scott, *A Greek Lexicon* (London: Oxford University Press, 1973), pp. 1076–77.

37. For both meanings of the word see Dionysius of Halicarnassus, *The Roman Antiquities* VII, 2, 4. For the latter meaning, Dio, *Roman History* LXIX, 23. 4. In this latter use, the word seems to be synonymous with *thelynomenos*, "behaving effeminately" or "playing the woman." Also see Diogenes Laertius, *Lives of Eminent Philosophers* VI, p. 65.

38. J. Moffat, *A New Translation of the Bible* (New York: Harper & Bros., 1935).

39. J. J. McNeill, *The Church and the Homosexual* (Kansas City: Sheed, Andrews and McMeel, 1976), p. 52; G. G. Findlay, "St. Paul's First Epistle to the Corinthians," *The Expositor's Greek Testament II*, ed. W. R. Nicoll (Grand Rapids: Eerdmans, 1967), p. 817; and Boswell, pp. 106–7.

164   THE CRISIS OF HOMOSEXUALITY

40. Among them, F. F. Bruce, *1 and 2 Corinthians* (London: Oliphants, 1971), p. 61; C. K. Barrett, *A Commentary on the First Epistle to the Corinthians* (New York: Harper & Row, 1968), p. 141; F. W. Grosheide, *Commentary on the First Epistle to the Corinthians* (Grand Rapids: Eerdmans, 1953), p. 140; W. F. Orr and J. Walker, *1 Corinthians, a New Translation Introduction with a Study of the Life of Paul, Notes, and Commentary* (Garden City, N.Y.: Doubleday, 1976), pp. 198–99; H. Conzelmann, *A Commentary on the First Epistle to the Corinthians*, trans. J. W. Leitch (Philadelphia: Fortress Press, 1975), p. 106.

41. Deissman, p. 164, n. 4.

42. See also Atkinson, p. 91, and P. M. Ukleja, "Homosexuality in the New Testament," *Bibliotheca Sacra* 140, 1983, pp. 350–51.

43. Boswell, p. 107; McNeill, p. 53.

44. Ibid., pp. 338–53.

45. J. H. Moulton and G. Milligan, *The Vocabulary of the Greek New Testament Illustrated from the Papyri and other Non-Literary Sources* (Grand Rapids: Eerdmans, 1963), p. 79.

46. D. F. Wright, "Homosexuals or Prostitutes? The meaning of ARSENOKOITAI" (1 Cor. 6:9, 1 Tim. 1:10), "Vigiliae Christiannae" 38, 1984, pp. 126, 129–30, 134, 136, 144–46. Also P. Zaas, "1 Cor. 6:9ff; Was Homosexuality Condoned in the Corinthian Church?" *Society of Biblical Literature 1979 Seminar Papers*, Vol. 2, ed. P. J. Achtemeier, SBL Seminar Papers Series, 14 (Missoula, Mont.: Scholars Press, 1979), pp. 208–09. Zaas rightly sees that the etymology of the word is "one who lies with a male," but goes on to claim, mistakenly, that the majority of occurrences are in Hellenistic moral and astrological literature and to connect the activity for the most part with idolatry.

47. Scroggs, pp. 108–9.

48. Conzelmann, p. 106.

49. Wright, p. 87.

50. J. R. W. Stott, "Homosexual Marriage: Why Same-Sex Partnerships Are Not a Christian Option." *Christianity Today*, Nov. 22, 1985.

CONCLUSION

Stanton L. Jones

How can any of us *dare* to condemn someone else for a sexual proclivity that they did not choose and that was caused by biological factors before birth?

How can any of us *dare* to condemn someone to a life of trying to change that which is unchangeable?

How can any of us *dare* to declare immoral a behavior so common and so controversial?

How can any of us *dare* to deny to someone else what we all crave for ourselves—to be united for life with another person who loves us?

Are there any *easy* answers to these questions? There are none—though there are answers. Part of what makes these questions so tough is that many of these and other questions asked by those supporting liberalization of the church's stand on homosexual behavior contain hidden assertions that are questionable but difficult to refute—such as the assertion that homosexual orientation is unchangeable.

The debate over homosexuality is deadly serious, and it is being played for high stakes. A substantial portion of our population detests homosexuals. In mild forms this comes out in "queer" jokes, teasing, stereotyping, and other forms of subtle cruelty that we are all so good at. In more advanced forms, this hatred takes the form of callous indifference toward the AIDS crisis, gay bashing, and explicit discrimination against homosexuals in housing and other life necessities.

On the other side, the gay-rights movement and those advocating what they call "gay liberation" are pushing to obliterate all sodomy laws, redefine the fundamental meaning of family, develop affirmative-action programs for homosexuals, and in many ways reshape our core understanding of religion and morality. My own professional organization, the American Psychological Association (APA), may soon consider a move to classify as unethical any professional offering services to help homosexuals overcome their homosexuality; since I have helped several in their process of change and intend to continue to hold this open as a possibility, a time could come in the not-too-distant future when I could be expelled from my professional organization for unethical behavior and thus perhaps be stripped of my license to practice clinical psychology. APA also seems to be moving toward "affirmative action" for gays, hoping to push higher-education departments that do not have homosexual faculty, such as mine at Wheaton College, to hire them. This possibility is not a hypothetical, academic issue.

Christianity Today recently published an essay on this topic, noting that behind the scenes in almost all denominations, homosexuality is called "The Issue." Advocates of gay liberation in many churches attempt to push at every opportunity any agenda that will broaden the definitions of morality and acceptable lifestyles; usually this is done in the endless string of committees and study groups on the topic of human sexuality that the denominations throw themselves into. Recently many Episcopalians were horrified when Bishop Spong, the self-described liberal bishop of Newark, ordained the first avowed gay-rights advocate and practicing homosexual as a priest. Spong picked this man because he felt he represented the perfect test case of a gay man committed to monogamous expression of his orientation. The man's lover of four years even participated in the ordination. One month later, the new priest publicly stated that monogamy was unnatural for all, gays and straights, and that we need to change our outmoded moral systems to reflect our real promiscuous natures. He was forced to resign from his ministry, Bishop Spong was disciplined, and the church was made to look foolish in the eyes of the world.

You cannot *not* take a stand on this issue. Fundamental issues are at stake. It is not that we should put a homosexuality clause in our denominational creedal statements, or that one's stand on homosexuality should become the new benchmark of orthodoxy, but what is at stake is not just a matter of how one reads a few Greek words. Rather, we find embedded in this painful, explosive issue matters that cut to the core of what we believe about life, faith, morality, and God.

Psychological and biological views
In the field of psychology, there is a loose cluster of somewhat objective standards of "mental health." By these standards, homosexuals are not usually judged disturbed, which rightly reflects the fact that most homosexuals are not miserable, dysfunctional, crazy people.

As a Christian, however, I believe there is a strong model of what a healthy human being is. We get that picture from the Bible, in what it proclaims conceptually, in the portraits of the only three sinless human beings ever to have lived (Jesus Christ and Adam and Eve before the Fall), and in the biblical portraits of the lives of the saints who were well along in their journey toward sanctification. But human failings and problems are not all labeled psychopathologies. There also will not always be agreement between Christian views and those of secular authorities.

What causes homosexuality is still uncertain. Nevertheless, there are two vital bits of information that must be understood: First, scientific thought moves in fads and is responsive to political and public opinion. We do not yet have hard proof for *any* causal hypothesis. Anyone who makes bold, confident claims is speaking with a confidence not supported by what we know at this point. We do not know what causes homosexuality—prenatal hormones may be involved, early childhood experience may be involved, critical life experiences may be involved.

Second, causation must be clearly thought out. A child dies, and we ask whose fault it was. The neighbor ran over the child with his car due to negligence; it was his fault 100 percent. Everyone breathes easier because life returns to its predictable shape where there is a clear cause for all that happens. But real life is not always so tidy. In psychology, causes are increasingly thought of in complex nets. The question is no longer "Was it genetic or early experience?" Rather, it is "What percentage of causation did genes contribute compared to experience and other variables?" Researchers can assign influence-weighting factors to many different variables, as when genetic factors are seen to contribute temperamental variables that in turn shape parental interaction processes that in turn influence school performance that in turn affect vocational opportunity and satisfaction that in turn predispose likelihood of engaging in criminal acts. Are we prepared to declare criminal behavior a nonmoral issue when the psychologists declare it to have a genetic component, because if we are, they are already there!

None of us approaches life with a clean slate and without encumbrances. Much of our behavior is shaped by forces beyond our control—genetics, physical conditions, parental influences, culture. But the biblical witness is that we are accountable, responsible, and that we are charged to do something about who we are. We shape who we are by the minute-by-minute decisions we make, building gradually who we become as men and women. The homosexual does not decide to be a homosexual, but then none of us decides to be who we are, either; depressed people do not decide to be that way, anxious people do not, narcissistic people, covetous or prideful people, suicidal people, alcoholics, adulterers, child molesters, criminals, sociopaths, and on and on—none of us decides to be any of these things.

But are we powerless? No. We do not make these grand decisions, but at a deceptively microscopic level, we decide the course, the trajectory of our lives. Within the bounds given to us (biological tendencies, family patterns, etc.), we make small decisions that have profound cumulative impacts upon who we become. It is mind boggling to consider that we may start with a genetic inheritance, a temperament, certain givens about the way our parents treat us, the environment we are exposed to, and so forth, but that building from this base we make small, and then larger and larger decisions that shape the course of our lives. I may not decide to become a dictatorial Hitler of a husband, but I did begin in childhood to decide how I thought of myself in relation to my mother, sister, and girls in the neighborhood. I decided how to treat the women I dated. I decided how much closeness I wanted with my wife; how much control I would demand in my marriage, whether I would take pride in or undermine the confidence of my wife. One decision builds upon another, which is why faithfulness in small decisions is so critical in the biblical view.

Therefore, is homosexuality caused by factors beyond voluntary control? Certainly few individuals make responsible adult decisions with no prior influence to go against nature and behave homosexually just for the "perverted" fun of it. But then few of us make deliberate decisions to be what we are, either. There is much beyond our ability to determine who we are because of what occurred at the Fall.

Change for homosexuals is possible. Every psychological study ever done has documented some change. But we must be careful about what we claim. Most responsible Christian ministries to homosexuals do not claim that they will reliably produce conversion to effortless heterosexuality. Rather, they aim to release strugglers from bondage to their homosexual patterns.

Are we condemning a person to a lifetime of deprivation and unhappiness if we suggest that celibacy is always available if people cannot reorient their attractions from homosexual to heterosexual? The view of many today in our sex-sated society is that maturity, health, and happiness are unavailable without genital sexual experience. The gay Episcopal priest I mentioned earlier, in the talk that resulted in his dismissal, asserted just this. When asked if he was saying that Mother Teresa would be advised to take a lesbian lover, he replied, "If you are asking me do I think that Mother Teresa ought to get laid, my answer is 'yes' " (*Newsweek*, Feb. 12, 1990, p. 61).

Clearly, by this standard, Jesus' life must be judged as immature and unfulfilled, as must all those Christian singles who take biblical morality with any degree of seriousness. There is no scientific evidence that people who do not experience regular genital sexual gratification, intercourse, are less well-adjusted than others. Such a position is clearly hostile to the whole of biblical revelation, where sexuality is viewed as a blessing given to *every* human being, and expression of that sexuality in the overt form of intercourse is reserved only for those who are married.

Homosexuality as an identity, as opposed to homosexual behavior, creates the naïve idea that homosexuality is a clear *thing*, an identity, and that you become that identity—a homosexual—as soon as you experience any homosexual feelings. One impulse—or regular impulses, or one experience, or even regular experiences—does not create an identity. Homosexual behavior occurs in every culture and in almost every animal species we know. But the concept of a homosexual *person*, where the homosexual orientation is stable, unchanging, and defines the person's very being, does *not* exist in any culture (see David F. Greenberg's *The Construction of Homosexuality* [Chicago: University of Chicago Press, 1988]).

As human beings, we not only categorize and define the world, but we do the same to ourselves. The notion of a homosexual, like the notions of an alcoholic or a schizophrenic, has not always existed and does not currently exist in every culture. We should be cautious about adopting the world's definition of identity for those struggling with these proclivities.

View of sin
We all tend to define reality in ways that make life easy and comfortable for ourselves; we are adept at this. One example that a number of folks have noted is the occurrence of "poor talk" among well-to-do yuppies—we are so disconnected from the poor by our own choice that we only have those more well-off than ourselves to compare ourselves to. When we make this comparison, we feel covetous; and to justify ourselves, we define our impulses to buy as "needs" rather than wants—I need that BMW, that car phone, that CD player, that fur coat, that microwave, that vacation trip in the Caribbean, that suit; and by convincing ourselves that we need

rather than merely want these things, we reduce our dissonance about consuming rather than acting as stewards of all that God has given us. Ezekiel 16:48–50 teaches us that it was this kind of materialistic greed and its complement of a lack of compassion and concern for the poor that were the most heinous sins among those that led God to destroy Sodom and Gomorrah. Note that we cannot conclude from this biblical account that God was positive or indifferent to the homosexual behavior of the people of these cities.

Similarly, isn't it comforting when we define sin as the deliberate, willful violation of an explicit clause in God's Law? By this definition, how many of us sin with any degree of regularity? Not many. In this way, we fall into the same trap as the religious folk Jesus criticized in his teaching as we excuse ourselves for not stealing when our lives are filled with covetousness, for not murdering when our lives are filled with jealousy and rage, for not committing adultery when our lives are filled with lust.

Many advocates for tolerance toward homosexuals take this stance, arguing that Paul in Romans 1 condemns those who engage in homosexual behavior because they act in rebellion against their own natures; in other words, they argue that those condemned in Romans 1 were heterosexuals engaging in homosexual behavior as rebellion against God. They argue that a contemporary homosexual, who engages in homosexual behavior precisely because it is *not* against his nature but rather fits perfectly with his or her nature, is therefore not sinning; he or she is not acting against her nature.

The biblical view of sin, however, is different. The most pervasive understanding of sin in the New Testament is that of "missing the mark," of falling short of God's intent for our lives. Who is our model of perfect righteousness? No one less than Jesus Christ himself. When we are less than what he was, when we are less than what we were meant to be in the garden, we are in sin. Sin infects and distorts all areas of life. The concept of sin does not imply that we are blameless when we have tendencies in a direction that we did not ask for. This is our common human dilemma—that we all have to struggle with desires and impulses and urges that arise unbidden. In fact, these urges feel normal to us. *Our sinful natures are in perfect accord with our character.* When we sin, it fits! It feels normal to treat other persons like property, to have contempt for others, to lust after others, and generally to fail to embody the beauty of character that Jesus manifested. It is for this reason that we all must cry out to the Father, "Lord, have mercy."

Just as we make life easy for ourselves in other areas, so also in the area of sin. Here we all have a fundamental solidarity with the people struggling with homosexuality. They are just like you and me. They have a desire to love and possess that which God forbids. To feel this way seems natural, and it arose seemingly without bidding. But all of us stand before the Holy One and find that we have missed the mark. The answer is not to amend the mark, as some do who claim that Christ himself or David or Jonathan were homosexuals, or that the early church did not realize the goodness of committed gay love. Nor is the answer to rage against God that we did not get to choose what we were ordained to struggle with. The answer is found in asking whether, given the cards that we have been dealt, we have handled rightly the gift of our lives. The answer to this for all of us is *no*. We have all made a shambles out of it.

Note the similar situation of the homosexual and the heterosexual single. Is sin only what is unnatural? I do not know many singles who don't struggle with their sexual feelings. We know that what feels natural in that case is not what would honor God. Some say this is not a fair comparison since heterosexual singles can always get married; to which I reply that there are more unmarried heterosexuals struggling with their sexuality who will *never* get married than there are homosexuals. The view of sin and the call of the gospel are the same for all. We can only normalize homosexual behavior by radically altering the historic Christian understanding of sin.

View of the call of the gospel

So, then, what are we to do? It is becoming increasingly common to view the call of the gospel as one of self-acceptance. A recent *Chicago Tribune* article about a gay church in the Chicago area said the core of its approach was that it meant to offer a place where people could feel accepted just as they are with no contingencies or expectations for change. Does the gospel exist to help us to feel good as we are? To accept and make us more the way we are naturally? That is an idea that appeals to many of us in our culture, but it is not the true gospel.

Are we indeed accepted by God just as we are? The Scriptures teach that God loves us passionately just as we are, that that love will never yield. But does God love what we are? Does he accept our natural definitions of our self-identities? The answer is clearly *no*. God hates sin. We do not deserve God's love, given who we are.

The call of the gospel is first to embrace the forgiveness offered through Christ for our sins. In reference to salvation, all sins are the same; we all stand guilty before God, guilty of having missed the mark. We stand outside of God's family because we are unworthy of being in that family. But God stands ready to embrace us and usher us back in if we will only ask for his forgiveness.

When we are forgiven, we are not merely enabled to be more of what we are already. Rather, God calls us forward into a journey; it is a journey of *becoming that which we naturally are not*. We are called to work out our salvation in fear and trembling, with the Holy Spirit working in and through us. We are called to a life of costly discipleship. We are called to a life of putting off the old man and putting on the new man (Eph. 4).

If I awake to the call of the gospel as a person who is consumed by that which is ultimately trivial, driven by my covetousness and greed to higher levels of conspicuous consumption, then I must embark upon becoming what I am not, a person whose life is transformed by grace into one characterized by clear, godly priorities, generosity, and contentment. If my life is consumed by anger, resentment, and bitterness, the gospel calls me to become what I am not, a person who is a gentle embodiment of forgiveness and forbearance, filled with gratitude for the manifold gifts, which I had been given.

Sexual intercourse is meant to be a life-uniting act between a woman and a man whose lives are knit together by marriage. The uniting of two very different bodies symbolizes and helps to bring about a more profound reality—the uniting of two lives. What should a married heterosexual do if he realizes that for him, sex is just gratification, just getting his jollies, that he is just "not into intimacy, sharing, sacrifice, oneness" in his marriage, that it "isn't natural"? He is called to become what he is not, called to respond to the claims of the gospel on his life to become an Ephesians 5 husband, who loves with the sacrificial love of Christ for the church.

If you are a single heterosexual, perhaps your life has been characterized by a passionate preoccupation with sexual experimentation, whether enacted in behavior or imagination. God would call you to thankfulness for your sexuality, and self-discipline in obedience to his law. Whether this discipline feels natural is irrelevant because the call is objective, based on the real life of a real Christ who lives, and who died for us. That call may mean a life of sexual abstinence, and there are not many people I know who say that always feels natural. But God rewards richly those who follow him, for his "yoke is easy" and he will be our companion and provider as we are his servants. There are riches and blessings in the chaste single life that often are overlooked or downplayed. Finally, the sexual pleasures do not compare to the wondrous glory he will share with us someday if we follow him faithfully.

The call to the Christian struggling with homosexual desires is the same: to become what you are not. God calls you to faithful obedience, which means sexual fidelity, commitment to growth, commitment to a body of believers, and faithfulness in allowing God the opportunity to intervene in your life.

View of compassion
It is easy to sentimentalize compassion. When you have young children, you have to realize that what they want is not always best for them because they often do not know all the relevant factors in their circumstances. Whether it is dietary issues of wanting to subsist on pizza and Fruit Wrinkles, or manner of dress—like our two-year old wanting to be unencumbered by clothes in the depths of winter—parents acting out of compassion have to go against the wishes of the child to do what is best for her or him.

Though it wounds our human pride, it is eternally true that God is the Heavenly Father and we are but children before him, even when we are our most wise and venerable. Compassion is only true compassion when it is grounded in a sure knowledge of what is ultimately good for us.

Thus, to use compassion as a ground to modify our understanding of the witness of God's revelation on the topic of sexuality is a grave error. Jeremiah 6:14 condemns those who "heal the wounds of my people lightly, saying 'Peace, peace' when there is no peace." The image here is of one so driven to make others feel better that they proclaim peace is at hand when the enemy is right outside the gates. To do this is not compassion; it is deception and destruction. It is not uncompassionate to say things that may cause another distress if those things we say are true, are said out of a true caring for the other, and are said in a manner that is kind, wise, and mindful of the other's readiness to hear.

Therefore, the starting point of compassion with persons struggling with homosexual impulses is the clear message that acting on those impulses is wrong, that forgiveness is available for sins that we all have committed, and that healing and growth is available to all who approach God with an earnest desire to be forgiven and healed. Healing and growth do not mean that God always heals us the way we want, but he always responds to our needs, and his response is always what is right for us.

Second, after retaining the integrity of our Christian witness in this area, we must make efforts to rid ourselves of our fears, aversions, and superiority feelings so that we can truly fellowship with and share the burdens of those with homosexual desires. Most persons I know with homosexual desires feel practically no freedom to ask others for prayer, to share about their struggles, to expect to be welcomed as a friend if they were to let others know about their problem. This is our fault. Christianity is not supposed to be a country club for the successful, a fraternity for the advantaged. It should be a hospital for the sick, a fellowship of the weak, a community of the needy. We need to wake up and realize that homosexuals are not fundamentally different from anyone else. There should be a level of comfort with and openness about this problem in our churches, which is rarely realized today.

Next, our compassion should lead us to care for the dying. A time is coming when the majority of those who suffer from AIDS in the West may no longer be homosexuals; but that is not currently the reality. We should collectively be active in ministry to this afflicted population. Some say compassion begins here in believing no one deserves to die, especially those who die horribly from AIDS. I believe the answer is exactly the opposite: Compassion begins with the realization that we all deserve to die and are thus no different from the person with AIDS, and that God calls us to a ministry of compassion and mercy to everyone and *anyone*.

None of us has done all that we could to advance the cause of the gospel in this day. And homosexuality is one of the major battle-fronts on which the church will either shame our Lord by our lack of courage, insight, and compassion, or reflect God's character and heart.

ABOUT THE AUTHORS

Darlene Bogle *is director of Paraklete ministries, an outreach group to the homosexual community in and around Hayward, California, and a staff minister at the Hayward Foursquare Church.* She has written Long Road to Love *(Chosen Books, 1985) and* Strangers in a Christian Land *(Chosen Books, 1990).*

Colin Cook *is cofounder of Homosexuals Anonymous and counsels in the area of recovery from homosexuality. He is also the founder and director of Quest Learning Center in Reading, Pennsylvania. He is the author of* Homosexuality: An Open Door? *(Pacific Press, 1984) and is a speaker on several tape albums that address freedom from homosexuality.*

Bob Davies *is executive director of the North American board of Exodus International and a staff writer with Love In Action, an ex-gay ministry, which has been part of Exodus since 1976. He is a graduate of Prairie Bible College. His articles have appeared in several magazines.*

Ronald Enroth *is professor of sociology at Westmont College in Santa Barbara, California. He is a graduate of Houghton College and the University of Kentucky, where he earned his Ph.D. in sociology. He has written several books, including* The Gay Church *(Eerdmans, 1974) and* The Lure of Cults and New Religions *(InterVarsity Press, 1987).*

Stanton L. Jones *is associate professor of the Department of Psychology at Wheaton College. He received his Ph.D. in clinical psychology from Arizona State University. He is a licensed clinical psychologist for the state of Illinois and the author of* Psychology and the Christian Faith: An Introductory Reader *(Baker Book House, 1986).*

Bernard J. Klamecki *is a physician and surgeon specializing in proctology in Milwaukee, Wisconsin. He is a graduate of the Marquette University School of Medicine.*

David Neff *is managing editor of* CHRISTIANITY TODAY *and director of the Christianity Today Institute. He is a graduate of Loma Linda University and Andrews University, and he has pursued additional graduate study at San Francisco Theological Seminary. Before coming to* CHRISTIANITY TODAY, *he served as editor of HIS, InterVarsity Christian Fellowship's erstwhile magazine for college students.*

Ronald M. Springett *is professor of New Testament Language and Literature at Southern College in Tennessee. He is a graduate of the University of Manchester in Great Britain, where he earned his Ph.D. in New Testament biblical criticism while studying under F. F. Bruce. He has written* Homosexuality in History and the Scriptures *(Biblical Research Institute, 1988).*

Tim Stafford *is senior writer for* CHRISTIANITY TODAY *magazine. His recent books include* The Sexual Christian *(Victor Books, 1989), the first book in* CT's *book series, and* Comeback *(Zondervan, 1990), the story of Dave Dravecky.*

John Stott *is president of Christian Impact and rector emeritus of All Souls Church, Langham Place, England. He is a graduate of Trinity College, Cambridge, England. He has traveled extensively, especially in Third World countries, speaking at seminars for pastors. He is the author of* Involvement *(Revell, 1985) and* The Cross of Christ *(Inter-Varsity Press, 1986).*

J. Isamu Yamamoto *is book editor for* CHRISTIANITY TODAY. *He is a graduate of Gordon-Conwell Theological Seminary. He has written* The Puppet Master: An Inquiry into Sun Myung Moon and the Unification Church *(InterVarsity Press, 1977) and* Beyond Buddhism: A Basic Introduction to the Buddhist Tradition *(InterVarsity Press, 1982).*